MODERN LEGAL STUDIES

QUASI–LEGISLATION:

Recent Developments in Secondary Legislation

D1423785

AUSTRALIA AND NEW ZEALAND
The Law Book Company Ltd.
Sydney : Melbourne : Perth

CANADA AND U.S.A.
The Carswell Company Ltd.
Agincourt, Ontario

INDIA
N. M. Tripathi Private Ltd.
Bombay
and
Eastern Law House Private Ltd.
Calcutta and Delhi
M.P.P. House
Bangalore

ISRAEL
Steimatzky's Agency Ltd.
Jerusalem : Tel Aviv : Haifa

MALAYSIA : SINGAPORE : BRUNEI
Malayan Law Journal (Pte.) Ltd.
Singapore and Kuala Lumpur

PAKISTAN
Pakistan Law House
Karachi

MODERN LEGAL STUDIES

QUASI–LEGISLATION:

Recent Developments
in Secondary Legislation

by

GABRIELE GANZ
Professor of Law,
University of Southampton

LONDON
SWEET & MAXWELL
1987

Published in 1987 by
Sweet & Maxwell Limited of
11 New Fetter Lane, London.
Computerset by Burgess & Son (Abingdon) Limited.
Printed in Great Britain by
Hazell, Watson & Viney Limited,
member of the BPCC,
Aylesbury, Bucks

British Library Cataloguing in Publication Data

Ganz, Gabriele
  Quasi-legislation: recent development in
  secondary legislation.—2nd. ed.—(Modern
  legal studies)
  1. Administrative law—Great Britain
  I. Title II. Ganz, Gabriele. Administrative
  proceedures III. Series
  344.102'6   KD4879

  ISBN 0–421–37020–3
  ISBN 0–421–29850–2 Pbk

PREFACE

When the idea for this book was first conceived the only literature on the subject was Megarry's pioneering note in the Law Quarterly Review of 1944 in which he coined the phrase, quasi-legislation. Later on the subject surfaced in text books such as Harlow and Rawlings, *Law and Administration* and Turpin's *British Government and the Constitution.* It was not until after the book was completed that the topic received the attention of the House of Lords in a short debate on "Codes of Practice and Legislation" (January 15, 1986). In that debate there was reference to the work of Baldwin and Houghton which was later published in Public Law ((1986 P.L. 239).

In that debate Lord Renton chronicled the population explosion in this area. Whereas in 1973 when his Committee on the Preparation of Legislation started their deliberations the development was still in its infancy, he found that since then there were 25 statutes under which 48 codes of practice could be made. At the time he was speaking Parliament was busily enacting further statutes under which codes of practices could be made and the very next day the House of Lords debated an amendment to the Animals (Scientific Procedures) Bill to give more legal force to the codes of practice under that Bill. This was eventually embodied in the Act. Conversely a few weeks later on February 24, 1986, the House of Lords defeated the Government on an amendment to the Local Government Bill which gave the code of practice under that Bill a purely advisory status. These debates highlighted the utter confusion about the legal status of such codes which was one of the main complaints in the debate on Codes of Practice and Legislation. This issue is addressed in Chapter 2.

The second issue which worried their Lordships was the deficiency in Parliamentary control, in particular Parliament's inability to amend such codes which is discussed in Chapter 3. The only positive concession wrung from the Government was a pledge that, where the provisions of a code were capable of affecting the outcome of legal proceedings, the Act would provide for it to be subject to the approval or annulment by Parliament.

A third complaint was the inaccessibility of this material.

Lord Campbell, who initiated the debate, paid tribute to government departments without whose help he could not have opened the matter. Unfortunately such help is not available to everyone. The paper chase involved in finding these documents is chronicled in Chapter 3.

The positive advantage of this development the ability to deal with detailed matters in non-technical language was also stressed. Most interestingly the role of codes in the realm of industrial relations was commended by one speaker as a step towards consensus, whilst the Code on picketing made under the Employment Act 1980 was condemned by other speakers because the limit of six imposed on the number of pickets should have been contained in the statute and because the Code, not being founded on goodwill, had suffered severe knocks during the miners' strike. This issue is discussed in Chapter 4.

The debate only touched in passing on the enormous mass of rules, discussed in Chapter 5, which are addressed to officials whether of central or local government or other public bodies. Codes of practice are only the tip of an enormous iceberg of quasi-legal rules.

The remedies proposed by their Lordships to structure this chaos were very similar to those put forward in the Conclusion. There was support for a Scrutiny Committee to look at codes and at draft Bills containing clauses providing for codes of practice. The Lord Advocate pointed out the practical and constitutional difficulties of this latter suggestion. Lord Renton even suggested an approved code of practice for preparing codes of practice. Lord Henderson suggested an Act equivalent to the Statutory Instruments Act 1946 for codes of practice and he also called for the Law Commission to examine this development, but the Lord Advocate in rejecting this proposal thought the remedy lay with Parliament itself when considering Bills which had provisions for codes of practice. The House of Lords is beginning to perform this task for which it is eminently suited by its constitutional function. Lord Campbell lamented that there was no book on this subject; what follows is intended to fill this gap, however inadequately.

September, 1986   Gabriele Ganz

CONTENTS

TABLE OF CASES

TABLE OF STATUTES

TABLE OF STATUTORY INSTRUMENTS

Chapter 1

INTRODUCTION

In 1944 in a seminal note Mr. Megarry (as he then was) coined the phrase "administrative quasi-legislation"[1] to describe law-which-is-not-a-law such as tax concessions and "Practice Notes" (the state-and-subject type) and administrative arrangements affecting the operation of law between one subject and another (the subject-and-subject type). Since that date there has been a population explosion of the former type of quasi-legislation, raising similar constitutional issues to those examined by the Committee on Ministers' Powers in relation to delegated legislation.[2]

Just as that Committee found great difficulty in delimiting delegated legislation, and particularly in distinguishing it from executive action,[3] so quasi-legislation is problematical because it is not a term of art. It is used here to cover a wide spectrum of rules whose only common factor is that they are not directly enforceable through criminal or civil proceedings. This is where the line between law and quasi-legislation becomes blurred because there are degrees of legal force and many of the rules to be discussed do have some legal effect. It is also not possible to draw a clear distinction between law and quasi-legislation on purely formal lines *i.e.* the mechanism by which it is made. A legally binding provision may be contained in a circular whilst a code of practice may be embodied in a statutory instrument. We draw the line at rules which have a limited legal effect at one end of the spectrum and purely voluntary rules at the other end. We are not concerned with self-regulation by private organisations except as an illustration of voluntary codes.

Within these parameters there has been an exponential growth of statutory and extra-statutory rules in a plethora of forms. Codes of practice, guidance, guidance notes, guidelines, circulars, White Papers, development control policy notes, development briefs, practice statements, tax concessions, Health Service Notices, Family Practitioner Notices, codes of conduct, codes of ethics and conventions are just some of the guises in which the

---

[1] (1944) 60 L.Q.R. 125.
[2] Cmd. 4060 (1932).
[3] *Ibid.* p. 19.

rules appear. One can only echo the cry of the Donoughmore Committee, "The most scientific explorer cannot make a map of a jungle."[4]

Nevertheless a map has been attempted. First, the extent to which such rules can have legal effect has been explored as has the constitutional implication of "a process whereby statutes may acquire an administrative gloss."[5] Then the safeguards are examined: parliamentary control, consultation, control by the courts, who have been very active in this area, by the Council on Tribunals and the Ombudsman and, above all, publication. Megarry wrote in 1944,

> "A system under which the practitioner may have to search Hansard, the Stationery Office list of official publications and the weekly law papers to find out how far up-to-date text-books and the statute book itself can be relied upon as stating the effective law will commend itself to few."[6]

He would have to look a great deal further afield today. The same remedy which was recommended by the Donoughmore Committee for improving oversight of delegated legislation is needed here *i.e.* a parliamentary scrutiny committee.

The most basic question explored is the rationale for this burgeoning of quasi-legal or purely voluntary rules. The issue with which we are concerned is not why there should be rules rather than discretion[7] but why quasi-legislation or non-legal rules should be preferred to law. To answer this question it has been necessary to examine the areas in which the rules operate and the functions they perform. They have been divided into those rules which are addressed to private individuals and those aimed at public bodies, such as local authorities, nationalised industries, health authorities, the police and the rules by which government departments structure their discretion as well as conventions. Similar practical reasons for such rules recur in each category of case, namely flexibility and lack of technicality. In some cases the issue is justiciability but the basic underlying reason for preferring quasi-legal or non-legal rules is that the voluntary acceptance of rules is better than their legal enforcement. Consensus is, therefore, the precondition for the effectiveness of such rules. This precondition has by no means always been fulfilled in the case of rules addressed to private individu-

[4] *Ibid.* p. 27.
[5] Megarry, *op. cit.* p. 127.
[6] *Ibid.* p. 128.
[7] See Davis, *Discretionary Justice* (1969).

als. It is also increasingly breaking down in the government's relations with public authorities. Some conventional rules are no longer being observed by either ministers or civil servants, a development which, if it accelerates, poses a threat to Britain's unwritten constitution.

Mr. Megarry thought quasi-legislation was somewhat of a curate's egg. Since then it has been used almost as a panacea. Hardly a statute is passed without a provision for a code of practice or guidance. Often this is the result of a political compromise between conflicting pressures to do nothing and to enact legal rules. Similarly, voluntary codes ranging from those dealing with advertising to straw burning are, in many cases, adopted to stave off legislation. However, the mere promulgation of a code does not ensure its observance, which needs to be monitored. There must be widespread acceptance in the absence of legal enforcement if the code is to be effective. Consensus cannot be created by issuing a code; a code can only work where it is based on consensus. If used in the proper context quasi-legislation can be more effective than law because it can draw on a reservoir of goodwill, acceptance and a sense of honour and responsibility which already exists, as well as having practical advantages over legislation. Used in the wrong context for reasons of political expediency such rules are still-born and bring the whole genus into disrepute.

Chapter 2

THE LEGAL EFFECT AND CONSTITUTIONAL IMPLICATIONS OF QUASI-LEGISLATION

Distinction between legal form and legal force. In the first place it is necessary to distinguish legal form from legal force. Law can be made by informal means as well as by statutes and statutory instruments. Conversely, the legal force of a provision is not *ipso facto* enhanced by embodiment in an Act or statutory instrument instead of in a less formal document. Legal force derives from statute or exceptionally prerogative and their interpretation by the courts.

Formally it is not difficult to distinguish Acts of Parliament as they are the outcome of a recognised procedure. However, exceptionally an Act may incorporate a White Paper in a schedule[1] thus giving legislative form to a non-legislative document. Statutory instruments are also clearly identifiable but Acts do not necessarily provide for delegated legislation to be made in this form or by any other formal procedure such as bye-laws. Thus the Road Safety Act 1967, s.7[2] gave the Secretary of State power[3] to approve a breath test device without specifying any particular method for giving his approval. His choice of a circular to implement this power led to problems of proof when the courts refused to accept the circular as evidence of his approval[4] and it was only when an Order had been made which was published by the Stationery Office but was also not a statutory instrument that the courts would take judicial notice of his approval.[5]

Similarly the exercise by circular of sub-delegated power to requisition land under the Defence Regulations gave rise to judicial strictures in *Blackpool Corporation* v. *Locker*[6] precisely because it was held to have the force of law without being subject to the safeguards of the Statutory Instruments Act 1946.

[1] Prices and Incomes Act 1966, Sched. 2.
[2] See now the Road Traffic Act 1972, s.8, as amended by Sched. 8 to the Transport Act 1981, which was brought into force by S.I. 1983 No. 576.
[3] This power was unsuccessfully challenged in *Hayward* v. *Eames, The Times*, October 10, 1984.
[4] *Scott* v. *Baker* [1968] 3 W.L.R. 796.
[5] *R.* v. *Clarke* [1969] 2 Q.B. 91; *R.* v. *Jones* [1970] 1 W.L.R. 16, and see now the Breath Analysis Devices (Approval) Order 1983.   [6] [1948] 1 K.B. 349.

Circulars are also used to issue directions which have the force of law under the Town and Country Planning General Development Order 1977.[7] The Prison Rules may confer a power to give directions on the Secretary of State and this will be exercised by Standing Orders which to that extent will have some legal force.[8]

A direction under the Industry Act 1975, s.7(1) was used to give statutory effect to guidelines to the National Enterprise Board.[9] Para. 2 of the 1976 Direction provided that the Board, "shall comply with the requirements relating to the Board which are printed in heavy type." An action for breach of statutory duty based on these guidelines was allowed to go to trial and an order to strike out the action was dismissed.[10] Under the Local Government Finance Act 1982, s.8 the Secretary of State may adjust the block grant payable to local authorities by reference to guidance issued by him. Similarly the Wildlife and Countryside Act 1981, s.50 provides that payments under management agreements shall be determined in accordance with guidance given by Ministers. More informal than any of these methods of law making was the Prime Minister's instruction, issued under article 4 of the Civil Service Order in Council 1982, prohibiting civil servants at G.C.H.Q. from belonging to a trade union.[11]

These examples illustrate that informal documents may have legal force; the converse, that the embodiment of informal documents in legislative form only gives them such legal force as the statute provides, is well illustrated by the Prices and Incomes Act 1966 which merely enjoined the National Board for Prices and Incomes to have regard to the White Paper contained in Schedule 2. When the first Police and Criminal Evidence Bill was being debated in Parliament in 1983, the Opposition urged the Government to put the codes of practice to be made under the Bill into a Schedule to the Bill.[12] This would of course have affected the way they were discussed in the House and, it was said, the language in which they were couched, though the Prices and Incomes Act 1966 set a precedent for incorporating a White Paper in informal language in an Act. But the Government were

---

[7] Circular 2/81, App.D.—direction for granting planning permission for development in contravention of a development plan.
[8] In *Raymond* v. *Honey* [1982] 2 W.L.R. 465, 470G, Lord Wilberforce left open whether they have any legislative force at all.
[9] Trade and Industry, December 24, 1976.
[10] *Booth & Co. (International)* v. *National Enterprise Board* [1978] 3 All E.R. 624.
[11] *C.C.S.U.* v. *Minister for the Civil Service* [1984] 3 W.L.R. 1174.
[12] Standing Committee J, col. 1001 *et seq.* (March 1, 1983).

correct in pointing out that the legal force of the provisions depended not on whether they were in the Act, a statutory instrument or a code of practice, but on the express provision in the Act which set out their legal effect.[13]

Just as embodying a code of practice in a statute does not *per se* enhance its legal status, so providing that it shall be contained in a statutory instrument does not enhance its legal effect. The Housing (Homeless Persons) Act 1977, s.5 provides for disputes between local authorities as to the housing of homeless persons to be determined in default of agreement in accordance with appropriate arrangements embodied in a statutory instrument by the Secretary of State. The statutory instrument[14] set out the Agreement on Procedures negotiated between the local authority associations. In *R.* v. *Eastleigh Borough Council, ex p. Betts*[15] it was held that the Agreement on Procedures did not impose a legally binding code on housing authorities but was merely a policy document.[16] *A fortiori* a provision that a code shall be approved by means of a statutory instrument (*e.g.* the Control of Pollution Act 1974, s.71) does not enhance its legal standing, which is as set out in the Act.[17]

It is clear then that, though one can distinguish formally between Acts, statutory instruments and other rule-making mechanisms, their legal effect can only be ascertained from statutory provisions and their judicial interpretation. There are degrees of legal force and these are not directly correlated to the procedure by which the provisions are made. Quasi-legislation is, therefore, not a term of art but a matter of degree.

The difficulty of distinguishing between quasi-legislation and delegated legislation is well illustrated by the Immigration Rules made by the Secretary of State under section 3(2) of the Immigration Act 1971. In *R.* v. *Chief Immigration Officer, ex p. Bibi*,[18] Roskill L.J. said, "These rules are just as much delegated legislation as any other form of rule-making activity or delegated legislation which is empowered by Act of Parliament." Lord Denning M.R. in *R.* v. *Home Secretary, ex p. Hosenball*[19] thought this went too far, "They are not rules in the nature of delegated legislation so as to amount to strict rules of law."

---

[13] See now Police and Criminal Evidence Act 1984, s.67.
[14] S.I. 1978 No. 69.   [15] [1983] 3 W.L.R. 397.   [16] p. 402G.
[17] s.60 and s.71. The Counter-Inflation Act 1973, s.2 provided that the Agencies set up under the Act must have regard to codes which were to be contained in statutory instruments.
[18] [1976] 1 W.L.R. 979, 985F.
[19] [1977] 1 W.L.R. 766, 780H–781B.

Geoffrey Lane L.J. thought that, "These rules are very difficult to categorise or classify. They are in a class of their own."[20] Cumming-Bruce L.J. reached the heart of the problem when he said,[21]

> " . . . they are not in my view in any sense of themselves of legislative force. It is true that by section 19(2) of the Immigration Act 1971 the rules are given legal effect in the field of the appellate process to the adjudicator or tribunal, which does not arise of course in connection with Mr. Hosenball's case. But the legal effect that the rules have in that limited field flows not from the fact that they have been published by the Minister and laid before both Houses of Parliament, but because by section 19(2) the rules are given an effect which is in a certain field clearly legally enforceable, and that is quite a different matter."

In other words, the rules are by statute made binding on the adjudicator and the appeal tribunal in that they must allow an appeal from the immigration officer if they consider that the decision was not in accordance with the rules but they are not made binding on the courts, though the courts must have regard to them on an application for judicial review to quash the tribunal's decision.[22]

The Immigration Rules are made binding on the adjudicators and tribunal by section 19(2) of the Immigration Act 1971. When the first Police Bill was being discussed in the House in 1983, it was suggested that the new clause relating to guidance by the Home Secretary to Chief Constables concerning discipline and complaints should provide for such guidance to be binding on police officers. This was rejected by the Government on the ground that, "It would be wrong if a Secretary of State were able to legislate by means of issuing guidance. That would create a third type of legislation in addition to subordinate legislation by Statutory Instrument, which is not what is involved."[23] As we saw above, such a third type of legislation already exists in the form of circulars, directions and guidance. If the argument that

---

[20] p. 785D.
[21] p. 788F–G. Lord Wilberforce in *R.* v. *Home Secretary, ex p. Zamir* [1980] 3 W.L.R. 249, 254B was surely going too far when he said that the rules have no statutory force.
[22] p. 781A.
[23] Standing Committee J, col. 1432, March 24, 1983. See now Police Act 1984, s.105.

binding guidance has the status of legislation[24] is correct this would also apply to the Immigration Rules which takes us back to Roskill L.J.'s statement in the *Bibi* case. This issue is largely one of terminology as legislative force is a matter of degree.

Legal effect of legislative codes. The propriety of giving legislative force to a code which was not embodied in legislation was discussed when the prototype of all codes, the Highway Code, was being debated in Parliament. An amendment was accepted making the Code subject to the approval of both Houses but this did not satisfy the critics, who felt that it should be embodied in a Schedule to the Bill or be drawn up by a Joint Select Committee.[25] The degree to which the Highway Code has legal force was set out in section 45(4) of the Road Traffic Act 1930,[26]

> "A failure on the part of any person to observe any provision of the highway code shall not of itself render that person liable to criminal proceedings of any kind, but any such failure may in any proceedings (whether civil or criminal, and including proceedings for an offence under this Act) be relied upon by any party to the proceedings as tending to establish or to negative any liability which is in question in those proceedings."

This provision has been held to create, "no assumption of negligence calling for an explanation, still less a presumption of negligence making a real contribution to causing an accident or injury. The breach is just one of the circumstances on which one party is entitled to rely in establishing the negligence of the other and its contribution to causing the accident or injury."[27] In *O'Connell* v. *Jackson*[28] it was said that, where the latest edition of the Code which for the first time gave advice on the wearing of crash helmets (though the previous edition printed this advice on the cover) was only issued a month before the accident, it was not necessary to establish that the latest edition was available to the plaintiff or that he had read it and that the latest edition could be adverted to for the limited purpose indicated by the above section.[29] The Highway Code which since 1968 contained the injunction, "Fit seat belts in your car and make sure they are

---

[24] *Ibid.*
[25] H.L. Deb., Vol. 75, col. 1514, *et seq.* (December 18, 1929).
[26] The latest provision is virtually identical, see Transport Act 1982, s.60.
[27] *Powell* v. *Phillips* [1972] 3 All E.R. 864, 868C (C.A.).
[28] [1971] 3 W.L.R. 463.
[29] *Ibid.* p. 467C.

always used" was prayed in aid to find plaintiffs who did not use them guilty of contributory negligence.[30]

The section giving legal force to the codes with respect to the Welfare of Livestock in the Agriculture (Miscellaneous Provisions) Act 1968 was closely modelled on the Road Traffic Act. Section 3(4) after providing that failure to observe a code shall not render a person liable to proceedings continues, "but such a failure on the part of any person may, in proceedings against him for an offence under Section 1 of this Act be relied upon by the prosecution as tending to establish the guilt of the accused . . . "[31] This provision was criticised by the Opposition as being one-sided and tilting the balance in favour of the prosecution.[32] The Parliamentary Secretary replied that failure to observe the codes could only assist the party making an allegation and a defendant making a counter-allegation which would not be apposite in the cases involving the welfare of livestock, in contradistinction—see O.E.D. to road traffic cases. But he also said that the defendant could always rely on compliance with the codes in his defence. This was queried on the ground that the codes could not be adduced as evidence unless the document had been in use for so long that the courts took judicial notice of it or the author of the document gave evidence. This was the ground on which the courts rejected the circular approving the *Alcotest* breathalyser.[33] In reply to this, it was argued that the law relating to evidence was broken in practice thousands of times a year. The clause survived intact after a division. Later Acts make express provision for the admissibility in evidence of codes of practice.

The provisions of the Health and Safety at Work Act 1974 follow these precedents but give somewhat greater force to codes of practice approved by the Health and Safety Commission than is the case with either the Highway Code or the Welfare of

---

[30] *Froom* v. *Butcher* [1975] 3 W.L.R. 379.

[31] " . . . unless it is shown that he cannot reasonably be expected to have observed the provision in question within the period which has elapsed since that provision was first included in a code issued under this section." This covers the specific case where the period between the time when the recommendation first appeared in the code and the apparent commission of the offence is regarded by the court as insufficient for the accused reasonably to be expected to have followed the recommendation. Similar provisions for codes of practice have been inserted into the Slaughter of Poultry Act 1967 by the Animal Health & Welfare Act 1984, s.7.

[32] Standing Committee B, col. 101 *et seq.* (December 5, 1967).

[33] *Scott* v. *Baker* [1968] 3 W.L.R. 796. Though this defect was cured when approval was contained in an Order published by H.M.S.O., see *R.* v. *Clarke* [1969] 2 Q.B. 91.

Livestock Codes. Section 17(2), after stating that failure to observe the code of practice does not render a person liable to civil or criminal proceedings but that it is admissible in evidence, then provides that,

> "if it is proved that there was at any material time a failure to observe any provision of the code which appears to the Court to be relevant to any matter which it is necessary for the prosecution to prove in order to establish a contravention of that requirement or prohibition that matter shall be taken as proved unless the court is satisfied that the requirement or prohibition was... complied with otherwise than by way of observance of the code."

This rebuttable presumption in favour of liability if a code is not observed was queried by the Opposition as fettering the court's discretion. The Government agreed to look at the matter again but was not impressed by the argument that the provisions went further than those relating to the Highway Code.[34]

So far there have been very few codes of practice approved by the Commission.[35] Their function has been to amplify regulations which tend to be couched in terms of general objectives and standards so as to be flexible rather than detailed and specific. Detailed guidance is then put into the code of practice but because of their legal status and the need for consultation, which is time-consuming, codes of practice take nearly as long to agree as regulations. Guidance notes which have no statutory status may, therefore, be used instead of or in addition to codes of practice. The Commission has a policy of dealing with particular hazards by a package of regulations, codes and guidance notes.[36] Enforceability will depend on where provisions are contained. This is well illustrated by the control limits for the exposure to asbestos dust. These were contained in guidance notes.[37] These limits were used by inspectors as part of their assessment of whether the requirements of the law, *i.e.* the Asbestos Regulations 1969[38] and the Health and Safety at Work Act 1974, which contains general obligations, have been complied with. It is now proposed[39] following E.C. Directives on

---

[34] Standing Committee A, col. 189, (May 9, 1974).
[35] 1981–1982; H.C. 400, (Evidence p. 80), Report of Employment Committee.
[36] *Ibid.* para. 10.
[37] See Guidance Note E.H. 10 (July 1984).
[38] S.I. 1969 No. 690.
[39] Consultative Document, *Control of Asbestos at Work*, Health and Safety Commission, H.M.S.O (1984).

Asbestos and the recommendations of the Advisory Committee on Asbestos to give these control limits statutory backing. The new Draft Regulations will contain control limits which may not be exceeded and the Approved Code of Practice will give practical guidance as to how these requirements can best be met. It is hoped that these absolute duties together with the enforcement policy which the Health and Safety Executive intends to pursue will result in better standards of protection for employees. Enforcement action is within the discretion of the Health and Safety Executive's inspectors who take into account not only guidance approved by the official bodies but also use codes drawn up by the industry itself to determine what is reasonably practical when enforcing the Act.[40] Though they do not have legal status they do have the weight attached to them, having regard to the nature of the organisation or the industry that has put them out.[41] Some industries would much prefer this form of self-regulation through their own codes to codes approved by the Commission[42] but this would be strongly contested by the T.U.C.[43] In view of this subtle gradation from statutory codes through notes of guidance to voluntary codes, it is not surprising that the C.B.I. complained to the Employment Committee that there was confusion about the status of codes of practice, guidance notes and industry's own codes.[44]

The codes of practice under the Control of Pollution Act 1974 are also given legal force in the context of enforcement of the Act. Section 72(6) provides that regard shall be had to the codes for minimising noise[45] in construing, "best practical means" so that magistrates' courts will have to take into account such codes where the Act provides that it is a defence to prove "that the best practical means have been used for preventing or for counteracting the effect of the noise."[46] By section 60(4) the local authority is enjoined to "have regard to the relevant provisions of any code of practice" for minimising noise before serving a notice imposing requirements to control noise from work carried out on construction sites. The codes may also be taken into account when local authorities are exercising their discretion under

[40] 1981–1982, H.C. 400, Q.32.
[41] *Ibid.* Q.35.
[42] *Ibid.* Evidence p. 19, Memorandum from the Chemical Industry.
[43] *Ibid.* Q.113.
[44] *Ibid.* para. 7.
[45] *e.g.* those dealing with ice cream van chimes, S.I. 1981 No. 1828, intruder alarms, S.I. 1981 No. 1829, and model aircraft, S.I. 1981 No. 1830.
[46] s.58(5) and s.59(5)—summary proceedings for noise nuisance.

section 58 to serve noise abatement notices and when magistrates' courts have to determine whether to make an abatement order under section 59 or whether an offence has been committed by a loudspeaker under section 62. As one of the codes stated, "The code of practice does not in itself create offences or have the force of law, but it is intended to be of assistance to local authorities and magistrates courts in the exercise of their powers and functions under Part III (Noise) of the Control of Pollution Act 1974. . . . "[47]

Under Part II of the Act it is a defence to a prosecution for pollution of a stream that it is in accordance with good agricultural practice and any practice recommended in a code approved by the Minister of Agriculture is deemed to be so.[48]

The legal effect of codes issued under the Employment Act 1980 was again defined so that they were not to give rise to any proceedings but were to be admissible in evidence before a court or industrial tribunal or the Central Arbitration Committee and "any provision of the Code which appears to the court, tribunal or Committee to be relevant to any question arising in the proceedings shall be taken into account in determining that question."[49] The two codes on Picketing and Closed Shop Agreements[50] which have been issued under this provision have given rise to major constitutional controversy. A majority of the Employment Committee regarded them as constitutionally undesirable and Mr. Enoch Powell called them "a species of unconstitutional legislation."[51]

The burden of the indictment is that the codes go beyond the terms of the existing statutes but as they have to be taken into account by courts as well as industrial tribunals they are a form of back-door legislation which has not been submitted to detailed line-by-line scrutiny as an Act of Parliament would be. They arose out of a political compromise between those who wanted the legislation to go further and those who wanted it to go less far than it did. The defence to this indictment by the Government and those who supported the codes was that they were made in accordance with the provisions of the 1980 Act which set out their legal status and that these provisions were modelled on those applicable to the Highway Code and the more recent provisions in the Employment Act 1975 giving A.C.A.S.

---

[47] Code of Practice on Audible Intruder Alarms, para. 1.3.—H.M.S.O. (1982).
[48] s.31(9).
[49] s.3(8).
[50] H.M.S.O. (1980), revised in 1983.
[51] 1979–1980; H.C. 822, para. 22.

power to issue codes of practice for promoting the improvement of industrial relations.[52] A similar duty to issue codes of practice for the purpose of promoting good industrial relations was contained in the Industrial Relations Act 1971[53] and the existing code was maintained in being with amendments by the Trade Union and Labour Relations Act 1974, Schedule 1 when the 1971 Act was repealed by the Labour government.[54] In rebuttal it was pointed out that the Highway Code dealt with less politically controversial matters, that the codes issued by A.C.A.S. under the 1975 Act were the result of consensus between both sides of industry and like the Industrial Relations Code under the 1974 Act would only be admissible before industrial tribunals and would not therefore bring industrial relations back into the courts. The argument against controversial codes invites the riposte that if the subject is not controversial there is no need for guidance.[55]

This brings us back to the use of such codes and whether they are constitutionally undesirable. The nub of the constitutional argument is that it is undesirable to embody in codes which have legal effect controversial provisions, which go beyond existing legislation because it is felt that legislation would be premature, but which may anticipate future legislation without going through the detailed scrutiny to which Acts of Parliament are submitted. The Highway Code, though it anticipated the legislation on seat belts, is only remotely analogous, as it stopped far short of making seat belts compulsory under the criminal law. The A.C.A.S. Codes, on the other hand, were reached by consensus, whilst the original Industrial Relations Code was controversial because of its association with the Industrial Relations Act which set up the Industrial Relations Court. It is not, however, their controversial nature which makes the codes constitutionally suspect, though it undoubtedly affects their practical operation. The constitutional argument hinges on the avoiding of legislation for reasons of political expediency. This is not of course confined to codes of practice. Statutory instruments may quite frequently be used in preference to statute to

---

[52] 1979–1980; H.C. 848,—Government Observations on the Employment Committee's Report.

[53] The provisions for an Industrial Relations Code were objected to on similar grounds by the Labour Opposition in the debates on the Industrial Relations Act 1971—see H.C. Deb., Vol. 810, col. 561, *et seq.* (January 27, 1971).

[54] This was the result of an amendment by the Conservative Opposition on which the Government were defeated, Standing Committee E, col. 57 (May 16, 1974).

[55] 1979–1980; H.C. 848.

evade close parliamentary scrutiny. But even this analogy is not exact because the codes do not just implement legislation. On crucial controversial issues such as limiting the number of pickets, secret ballots before taking industrial action and review of closed shop agreements, the codes have provisions which go beyond those of the Act. A court during the miners' strike granted an injunction that no more than six people (the figure mentioned in the Code) should be allowed to picket[56] thus giving the Code legal force and confirming the fears of back-door legislation. Even more worrying were the specific provisions, for example, about review of existing closed shop agreements which were deliberately omitted from the 1980 Act but included in the Employment Act 1982,[57] though their operation was postponed until November 1984.[58] The revised code of practice issued in 1983[59] dealt with the provisions as though they were already in force. It is this pre-emption of law by quasi-law which is the novel feature of these codes and constitutionally suspect. The codes have been defended as part of the "step-by-step" approach to industrial relations, though the Institute of Directors saw them more as a necessary evil and called for regular reassessment to determine whether their provisions should be incorporated into statute.[60] The codes are therefore not just back-door legislation but anticipatory legislation. They have not created consensus but confusion.

Though the use to which the codes under the Employment Act 1980 were put was constitutionally novel, the provision which gave them legal effect was clearly modelled on that contained in the Industrial Relations Act 1971 and the Employment Protection Act 1975,[61] with the difference that they were admissible in courts as well as tribunals. What then is their legal force? In *Lewis Shops Group* v. *Wiggins*[62] Sir Hugh Griffiths stated the position of the National Industrial Relations Court in relation to the Code under the 1971 Act thus,

> "But even in a case in which the code of practice is directly in point, it does not follow that a dismissal must as a matter of law be deemed unfair because an employer does not follow the procedures recommended in the Code.... The

---

[56] *Thomas* v. *NUM* [1985] 2 W.L.R. 1081, 1113.
[57] s.3.
[58] s.22.
[59] Brought into operation by S.I. 1983 No. 584.
[60] 1982–1983; H.C. 197i, p. 22.
[61] See also Race Relations Act 1977, s.47 and Sched. 4, para. 1.
[62] [1973] I.C.R. 335.

code is, of course, always one important factor to be taken into account in the case, but its significance will vary according to the particular circumstances of each individual case."[63]

This leaves tribunals with a great deal of discretion as to the weight which they attach to the code.

An analogous formula is used in relation to codes of guidance in statutes which provide that an administrative body "shall have regard" to such guidance. In *de Falco* v. *Crawley Borough Council*[64] Lord Denning M.R. interpreting section 12 of the Housing (Homeless Persons) Act 1977[65] said,

"But I am quite clear that the code should not be regarded as a binding statute. The council, of course, had to have regard to the code...but, having done so, they could depart from it if they thought fit. This is a case in which they were perfectly entitled to depart from it."[66]

The same formula was used in the Police Act 1976 in relation to the Police Complaints Board which "shall have regard to any guidance given to them by the Secretary of State with respect to such matters affecting the preferring and withdrawing of disciplinary charges as are for the time being the subject of guidance by him to chief officers of police..."[67] In *R.* v. *Police Complaints Board, ex p. Madden and Rhone*[68] a decision of the Board not to recommend disciplinary proceedings was challenged on an application for judicial review because they regarded themselves as bound by the Secretary of State's guidance to avoid "double jeopardy." McNeill J. *held* "that the board was in error in regarding the Guidance as something with which it was obliged to comply."[69] Thus a tribunal or body which

---

[63] *Ibid.* p. 338—see *British Labour Pump Co. Ltd.* v. *Byrne* [1979] I.C.R. 347 for the "no difference rule," *i.e.* that on the balance of probabilities the employers would have taken the same course had a proper procedure been followed. This decision will not be applied to fundamental defects of procedure—*Woodroffe* v. *British Gas Corporation*, December 2, 1985 (C.A.).

[64] [1980] 2 W.L.R. 664.

[65] "In relation to homeless persons...a relevant authority shall have regard in the exercise of their functions to such guidance as may from time to time be given by the Secretary of State." Before 1977 the non-statutory circular was held to be a relevant consideration within the *Wednesbury* case, *Bristol District Council* v. *Clark* [1975] 1 W.L.R. 1443.

[66] p. 673 H.

[67] s.3(8); see now Police and Criminal Evidence Act 1984, s.105.

[68] [1983] 1 W.L.R. 447.

[69] p. 471 F.

has to take a code of guidance into account must not then regard itself as bound by the guidance and can give it such weight as it thinks fit but it would not be entitled to ignore it completely.

Codes having indirect legal effect. Purely non-statutory guidelines may attain the same status by virtue of being relevant considerations to which those exercising discretion must have regard. This would seem to be the position with regard to planning circulars issued by the Department of the Environment.[70] They are not legally binding but they must be taken into account by local authorities, inspectors and the Secretary of State himself when exercising their discretion where such a circular is relevant. This follows from the *Wednesbury* principles[71] even in the absence of an express statutory provision to have regard to all material considerations.[72] A local authority may refuse to follow a circular, but, if it does so, (unless the circular conflicts with an existing statute) it is likely to be reversed on appeal, where there is one, and an inspector's recommendation in similar circumstances would not be acceptable to the Minister. The courts seem to accept that in these cases the circulars may be treated as binding by the local planning authority[73] or inspector. However, the Secretary of State cannot fetter his own discretion by laying down a policy.[74] He must always be prepared to depart from it. This rule applies to all bodies exercising discretionary powers in accordance with self-imposed policies or guidelines.[75]

Non-statutory codes and guidelines may also be given legal effect by making a grant or renewal of a licence conditional upon compliance with such a code and attaching conditions based on a code to the licence. This has been the mechanism used for the registration of private residential care and nursing homes. The Government commissioned two codes of practice from non-statutory bodies but expects those with responsibilities for registration to have regard to the codes when exercising their

---

[70] See Nott and Morgan [1984] J.P.L. 623. In *Bristol District Council* v. *Clark* [1975] 1 W.L.R. 1443 the same status was accorded to a housing circular.
[71] *Associated Provincial Picture Houses Ltd.* v. *Wednesbury Corporation* [1948] 1 K.B. 223.
[72] Town and Country Planning Act 1971, s.29(1).
[73] *R.* v. *Worthing B.C., The Times,* November 22, 1983.
[74] *British Oxygen Co. Ltd.* v. *Board of Trade* [1971] A.C. 610.
[75] *R.* v. *Eastleigh B.C., ex p. Betts* [1983] 3 W.L.R. 397.

discretion under the Registered Homes Act 1984.[76] Similarly the Minister of Agriculture announced that registration for manufacturers or dealers in medicated feeding stuffs for animals[77] would be made conditional on the signing of an undertaking that the dealer will comply with a code of practice drawn up by representatives from the trade associations. By this means purely voluntary codes can be incorporated into legal provisions.

Another mechanism for indirect enforcement is contained in the Independent Broadcasting Authority Act 1973. Section 9 gave the Independent Broadcasting Authority the duty to draw up a code governing advertising standards and gave it power to issue directions to programme contractors to secure compliance with provisions of the code. It also has the duty to draw up a code of guidance in regard to the showing of violence and other matters it considers suitable.[78] The contract between the I.B.A. and the programme contractors must contain such provisions as the Authority thinks necessary or expedient to enforce compliance with requirements imposed under the Act in relation to programmes.[79] The Act thus expressly makes contract the vehicle for enforcing compliance with codes drawn up under the Act.

This was also one of the mechanisms by which the Labour Government enforced its pay policy contained in its White Paper, *The Attack on Inflation*.[80] Its 1977 White Paper stated,

> "Where a firm has reached a settlement which is quite clearly inconsistent with the policies set out in the White Paper, the Government will take this into account in its public purchasing policy and placing of contracts and also in consideration of industrial assistance."[81]

The legality of taking into account its pay policy when entering into contracts was not seriously questioned and the enforcement of the Fair Wages Resolution[82] of the House of Commons by this mechanism was directly analogous. The controversy about the blacklist of companies centred round the legality of refusing

[76] Standing Committee B, col. 387, (March 29, 1983), Health and Social Services and Social Security Adjudications Bill. Local authorities are to regard the guidance as analogous to that issued under the Local Authority Social Services Act 1970, s.7.

[77] Animal Health and Welfare Act 1984, s.13, and see also s.14.

[78] s.5.

[79] s.13.

[80] See *Comment* [1978] P.L. 333.

[81] Cmnd. 6882.

[82] H.C. Deb., Vol. 427, col. 619 (October 14, 1946). The Resolution was rescinded in 1983.

selective industrial assistance provided under statutory powers and about the way in which the policy was administered. The controversy over the pay policy sanctions has close analogies with that over the codes under the Employment Act 1980. In each case a highly controversial set of rules which had for political reasons not been embodied in legislation was given legal force indirectly, in the former case by express statutory provision and in the latter by the use of discretionary power. This led to accusations of back-door legislation and misuse of power, which though not legally justified, do bring into question the constitutional propriety of by-passing Parliament.[83]

The same charge was made against the Labour Government when it tried to achieve comprehensive schools reorganisation by Circulars 10/65 and 10/66.[84] The first circular to local education authorities from the Labour Government recommended a variety of models for abolishing selection to schools and reorganising them on comprehensive lines and requested L.E.A.s to submit plans but contained no sanctions. The second circular advised local education authorities that approval for new projects in school building programmes would be refused if incompatible with the introduction of comprehensive education. The threat to challenge the legality of withholding approval for capital expenditure to implement an education policy which had not been endorsed by Parliament never materialised. A subsequent Labour Government finally legislated to enable it to force recalcitrant education authorities to submit plans for comprehensive reorganisation.[85] Again we see in this case of comprehensive education reorganisation an example of non-legal rules being given indirect legal effect followed by legislation which makes them legally enforceable. The charge is one of back-door legislation. The constitutional reasons are, however, somewhat different from the previous illustrations. Parliament was used as a weapon of last resort when persuasion backed up by financial sanctions had failed. To postpone the use of law or dispense with it altogether is, as we shall see, the main rationale for the development of quasi-law.

Law as backstop. The Local Government, Planning and Land Act 1980 contains an illustration where a statute itself provides for legal rules as a back-stop if codes of practice are not complied

---

[83] For a different critique of the constitutional problem raised by the "blacklist"—see Daintith, *Journal of Law & Society*, p. 218.
[84] H.C. Deb., Vol. 705, col. 415 (January 21, 1965).
[85] Education Act 1976, ss.1–3.

with by local authorities. Section 2 gives the Secretary of State power to issue codes of recommended practice as to the publication of information by local authorities about the discharge of their functions.[86] In section 3 he is given the power to make regulations by statutory instrument requiring authorities to publish information specified in the codes in the manner and form specified there if in his opinion it is necessary to make such regulations. This is a statutory provision for the use of law as a reserve power if a code of practice is not voluntarily obeyed.

The absence of a legal reserve power to back up the codes of practice for sites of special scientific interest under section 33 of the Wildlife and Countryside Act 1981 was strongly criticised in both Houses of Parliament during the passage of the Bill. The section was introduced by the Government in the House of Lords in response to pressure but the Government firmly rejected any form of compulsion in order to obtain the co-operation of the farming community except for those exceptional areas where the Secretary of State makes an order under section 29, which provides legal powers over the land subject to compensation. However, at a late stage of the Bill, an amendment was inserted in the House of Commons modelled on section 29 making it obligatory for the owner who has been notified of such a site of special scientific interest on his land to give notice if he proposes to carry out operations on the land likely to damage the flora and fauna and wait for three months or obtain the consent of the Nature Conservancy Council.[87] Breach of this provision is a summary offence.[88] But this provision could be sterilised by the amendment introduced simultaneously which made it obligatory for the N.C.C. to give the owner three months notice of the proposal to designate the area as one of special scientific interest in order to enable representations to be made, so giving the irresponsible landowner the opportunity to destroy the site.[89] The code of practice[90] which discouraged such conduct could not be enforced. This loophole has now been closed by the Wildlife and Countryside (Amendment) Act 1985. The duty of the landowner not to carry out operations now runs

---

[86] See D.O.E. circulars 14/80, 3/81, 24/81 and 28/83.

[87] s.28(5) or enters into an agreement under s.16 of the National Parks and Access to the Countryside Act 1949. The period is now four months; see the Wildlife and Countryside (Amendment) Act 1985, s.2.

[88] s.28(7).

[89] s.28(2). Compare the procedure for s.29 orders which take effect on being made but are then subject to challenge (Sched. 11).

[90] Code of Guidance on Sites of Special Scientific Interest, H.M.S.O. (1982).

from the date of notification to the owner that the area is one of special scientific interest. The notification no longer has to be preceded by a three months' period for making representations; instead this period now follows the notification.[91]

A "dispensing" power. Quasi-law may be used to confer benefits as well as impose duties. The White Paper containing the Criminal Injuries Compensation Scheme[92] can be put into this category. In *R.* v. *Criminal Injuries Compensation Board, ex p. Lain*[93] its genesis was held to be the royal prerogative but compensation is entirely *ex gratia*. Though the scheme gave no applicant a right of action to sue for compensation, Lord Diplock said it had legal effect. "It makes lawful a payment to an applicant which would otherwise be unlawful."[94] But, as he said earlier, it was the annual Appropriation Act which legalised the expenditure in the first place. "The only limitation upon the power of the executive government to confer benefits upon subjects by way of money payments is a practical one, to wit, the necessity to obtain from Parliament a grant-in-aid for that purpose."[95]

The conferring of benefits may not require an Appropriation Act but take a negative form *i.e.* by exempting the subject from a tax by means of an extra-statutory concession. The legal status of such concessions, which may apply to a class of taxpayer or to a particular individual, have much exercised the courts. They have been castigated as a violation of the Bill of Rights 1689 which made the Crown's pretended power of suspending and dispensing with laws illegal. But they have also been praised as practically convenient. No taxpayer can enforce a concession directly[96] or use it as a defence for non-payment of tax. They have come before the courts indirectly when third parties have tried unsuccessfully to make the Revenue collect the tax which they have waived. Such attempts have failed because of the absence of *locus standi*.[97] The concessions have also been prayed

---

[91] s.2.
[92] Cmnd. 2323 (1964).
[93] [1967] 3 W.L.R. 348.
[94] p. 363 E.
[95] p. 362 A.
[96] *e.g.* see Cmd. 8103 (1950) Appendix. If, however, a concession is construed as a representation not to levy a tax or to remit a tax, its breach may now give rise to judicial review for unfairness; see *R.* v. *I.C.R., ex p. Preston* [1985] 2 W.L.R. 836.
[97] *R.* v. *Commissioners for Customs and Excise, ex p. Cook* [1970] 1 W.L.R. 450. See now *R.* v. *I.R.C., ex p. National Federation of Self-Employed* [1981] 2 W.L.R. 722.

in aid for or against a particular interpretation of the statute. It was in this context that concessions were castigated in the *Vestey* Case[98] and the Revenue's attempt to make their interpretation of the Act more palatable in this way was rejected.

Similarly in *Absalom* v. *Talbot*[99] it was the taxpayer who sought to rely on a concession to support his interpretation of the Income Tax Act but this was also rejected by the court. Du Parcq L.J. said, "It might be well if this method were given statutory sanction, but, in my opinion, the fact of its adoption without such sanction cannot affect our decision in this case."[1] Scott L.J. posed the question "Is the practice (a) lawful; (b) devoid of legal sanction; or (c) contrary to law and therefore prohibited?"[2] He did not answer his own question in his powerful peroration,

> "No judicial countenance can or ought to be given in matters of taxation to any system of extra-legal concessions. Amongst other reasons, it exposes revenue officials to temptation, which is wrong, even in the case of a service like the Inland Revenue, characterised by a wonderfully high sense of honour. The fact that such extra-legal concessions have to be made to avoid unjust hardships is conclusive that there is something wrong with the legislation."[3]

This philippic is more concerned with the desirability than the legal force of tax concessions. It would seem that (b), devoid of legal sanction, describes concessions most accurately. They exist in a legal limbo. They have no legal basis and cannot be enforced by the taxpayer nor can they be prohibited. A concession is an immunity from being taxed which cannot be enforced or challenged. Whether they are constitutionally desirable is a different question.

It is clear that Scott L.J. thought that concessions were the outcome of bad legislation for which there is an obvious remedy. Viscount Radcliffe made the point explicit in *Inland Revenue Commissioners* v. *Frere*,[4] "I have never understood the procedure of extra-statutory concessions in the case of a body to

[98] *Vestey* v. *Inland Revenue Commissioners* [1979] 3 W.L.R. 915, 925E–926C and 945 A *et seq.* and [1978] 3 W.L.R. 693, 698H *et seq.*
[99] [1943] 1 All E.R. 589.
[1] p. 603 A.
[2] p. 593 H.
[3] p. 598 A.
[4] [1964] 3 W.L.R. 1193, 1209.

whom at least the door of Parliament is opened every year for adjustment of the tax code." The answer came from Sir Geoffrey Howe when he was giving evidence to the Treasury and Civil Service Committee on Budgetary Reform about the need for more than one Finance Bill because of the pressure of space. "For example, there are many extra-statutory concessions which have existed over many years which I am sure Committees here have said ought to be embodied in Statute but which it is extremely difficult to find time for."[5] It would seem, therefore, that so far as class concessions are concerned the reason for not embodying them in legislation is purely practical.[6]

Concessions to individual taxpayers usually on grounds of equity or hardship raise more difficult issues. Like all discretionary powers they are, as Scott L.J. pointed out, open to abuse. But constitutionally the dispensing power exercised by the Revenue in respect of tax is closely analogous to the exercise of discretion not to prosecute for an offence. In *R.* v. *Inland Revenue Commissioners, ex p. National Federation of Self-Employed*[7] the Inland Revenue gave a tax "amnesty" to the Fleet Street casual workers as part of an arrangement enabling them to collect tax in the future. Lord Roskill said, "No question of any dispensing power is involved ... On the contrary, their whole case was that they had made a sensible arrangement in the overall performance of their statutory duties in connection with taxes management."[8] If a tax amnesty is interpreted in this way, the same interpretation must apply *a fortiori* when the Inland Revenue temper the wind to a shorn taxpayer by an individual concession. The fact that discretion can be abused is not an argument against its existence but an argument for proper safeguards.

Conventions. Tax concessions are not often regarded as having a common denominator with constitutional conventions but in each case a legal rule is qualified and restricted in practice by an extra-legal rule. In each case the non-legal rule cannot by definition be enforced in the courts but the courts have given judicial countenance to conventions unlike extra-statutory concessions. In *Att.-Gen.* v. *Jonathan Cape Ltd.*[9] the convention of collective responsibility was held to give rise to an obligation of confidence which could be enforced by the courts. In *Carltona*

---

[5] 1981–1982; H.C. 137, Q. 500.
[6] See further, *infra* p. 93.
[7] [1981] 2 W.L.R. 722.
[8] p. 756 C.
[9] [1975] 3 W.L.R. 606.

Ltd. v. *Commissioner of Works*[10] the convention of individual ministerial responsibility was fundamental to the court's decision that officials could make decisions which constitutionally remained the decisions of the Minister. Again in *Ibralebbe* v. *The Queen*[11] the constitutional convention relating to the Judicial Committee of the Privy Council was relevant to the court's decision that the order in Council giving effect to a report of the Judicial Committee was a judicial order and the power to make such an order was, therefore, not abrogated by the granting of independence to Ceylon. In *Liversidge* v. *Anderson*[12] the court prayed in aid the convention of Ministerial responsibility to bolster its interpretation of Defence Regulation 18B. But in no case did constitutional conventions play a more important role than in *Re Constitution of Canada*[13] where the Canadian Supreme Court was asked *inter alia* to rule on whether there was a convention that the Canadian Parliament will not request the British Parliament to amend the Constitution of Canada without the agreement of the Provinces. The contention that such a question was not justiciable but a purely political issue was rejected by the Court. "Nor are we asked to enforce a convention. We are asked to recognise if it exists. Courts have done this very thing many times in England and the Commonwealth to provide aid for and background to constitutional or statutory construction."[14] The court then quoted several cases including those previously mentioned. In the course of a detailed analysis of the nature of conventions the majority of the court said,

> "Perhaps the main reason why conventional rules cannot be enforced by the courts is that they are generally in conflict with the legal rules which they postulate and the courts are bound to enforce the legal rules. The conflict is not of a type which would entail the commission of any illegality. It results from the fact that legal rules create wide powers, discretions and rights which conventions prescribe should be exercised only in a certain limited manner, if at all."[15]

They went on to add, "It should be borne in mind, however,

[10] [1943] 2 All E.R. 560.
[11] [1964] 2 W.L.R. 76.
[12] [1942] A.C. 206.
[13] [1982] 125 D.L.R. (3d.) 1.
[14] p. 88.
[15] p. 85.

that, while they are not laws, some conventions may be more important than some laws."[16] This was certainly borne out by the result of the case itself which held that whilst the Canadian Parliament's request had broken no laws it was in breach of a constitutional convention and as a result of this judgment major concessions were made by the Federal Government leading to the agreement of every Province except Quebec. Thus at the highest level, non-legal rules in conflict with the law itself, far from being regarded as unconstitutional, are the most important part of the constitution.

Conclusion. The foregoing discussion has shown that the line between law and quasi-law is blurred. Not only may informal instruments like circulars be legally binding but the bindingness of statutes and statutory instruments is a matter of degree. A statute may contain guidelines to which regard must be had by certain bodies and these will have no greater force than if they were contained in a code of practice. Again the embodiment of codes in statutory instruments does not give them greater force. The legal effect of a provision in whatever form can only be ascertained from the statute under which it is made and its judicial interpretation. The formulae vary but their common denominator is that breach of the provision does not give rise to legal proceedings but shall be taken into account by the relevant judicial or administrative body.

Purely non-statutory guidelines may be given the same legal effect by the application of the *Wednesbury Corporation* principles so that they have to be taken into account as relevant considerations but must not be treated as binding. They may also be given legal force by making compliance a condition for the granting or renewal of a licence or by making a contract conditional on observance of such rules.

Quasi-legislation has been attacked as unconstitutional legislation where rules are laid down in a controversial area going beyond the existing law and are given legal force either directly by statute (*e.g.* the Employment Act 1980) or indirectly through the exercise of administrative discretion (*e.g.* inflation and comprehensive education policies), because it is impolitic to legislate. These cases have been castigated as back-door legislation.

Conversely, Parliament is usurped where statutory powers and duties are not exercised in accordance with extra-statutory rules, *e.g.* tax concessions. But where the powers are prerogative

[16] p. 87.

ones their non-exercise in accordance with conventions is the lynch-pin of our constitution. It is not, therefore, quasi-legislation *per se* which is objectionable but that the use to which it is put may be constitutionally suspect and the controls over its exercise may leave much to be desired. These safeguards will now be discussed.

Chapter 3

CONTROL OVER QUASI-LEGISLATION

Since quasi-legislation is a substitute for legislation it is appropriate to start with an examination of what control Parliament has over the making of rules.

Parliamentary control

Where the rules are made under statutory authority, the provisions for parliamentary control are to be found there. An Act may provide that a code of practice to which regard must be had shall be contained in a statutory instrument[1] or shall be approved by a statutory instrument which is then subject to the parliamentary procedure specified in the Act. The Control of Pollution Act 1974, s.71 so provides in the case of codes of practice for minimising noise and makes the statutory instruments subject to negative resolution.[2] More frequently an Act provides for codes of practice to be brought into operation by statutory instrument as is the case for the codes made under the Employment Acts 1975[3] and 1980,[4] the Race Relations Act 1976[5] and the Police and Criminal Evidence Act 1984.[6]

But an instrument does not need to be a statutory instrument to be subject to parliamentary procedure.[7] Codes of practice or draft codes of practice may be subject to affirmative or negative resolutions in both Houses. Those subject to affirmative resolution include the codes under the Police and Criminal Evidence Act 1984,[8] the Welfare of Livestock Codes,[9] the Industrial Relations Code,[10] some of the codes made under the Employ-

---

[1] Counter-Inflation Act 1973, s.2(3).
[2] s.104.
[3] s.6(8).
[4] s.3(5).
[5] s.47(7).
[6]. s.67(4).
[7] The reverse argument adopted by Roskill L.J. in *R.* v. *Chief Immigration Offices, ex p. Bibi* [1976] 1 W.L.R. 979 that, because the Immigration Rules were subject to annulment they were delegated legislation in the full sense, is a *non sequitur.* They have the force given them by the Act—see *supra* p. 6 *et seq.*
[8] s.67(5).
[9] Agriculture (Miscellaneous Provisions) Act 1968, s.3(2).
[10] Trade Union and Labour Relations Act 1974, s.2(3), Sched. 1.

ment Act 1975[11] and those under the 1980 Act,[12] as well as those
made under the Wildlife and Countryside Act 1981.[13] Only
certain codes made under the Employment Act 1975 are subject
to affirmative resolutions, the rest are subject to annulment.[14]
This is also the case in respect of the Race Relations Code,[15] the
Immigration Rules[16] and the codes under the Mental Health
(Amendment) Act 1982[17] in relation to admission and treatment
of patients and those under the Health and Social Services and
Social Security Adjudications Act 1983[18] with regard to access to
children in the care of local authorities.

The main difference between parliamentary proceedings on
an Act and that on an affirmative resolution is not just the time-
limit on the debate of the latter but the lack of line-by-line
scrutiny and power of amendment.[19] The Employment Committee have more than once expressed concern that codes which
have not been through such a procedure should have quasi-legal
effect.[20] In the case of the Race Relations Code this stricture
evoked the response from the Employment Secretary that as the
code could not extend the law or create new offences,[21] it was
appropriate that the procedure relating to delegated legislation
should be followed.[22] He did, however, express concern that the
Secretary of State only has power to approve or reject the draft
codes prepared by the Commission for Racial Equality and
could not amend them to reflect the views of Government and
Parliament. The Prime Minister later announced that legislation
would be introduced to make this possible.[23] A similar result
was, however, achieved in this case by the Secretary of State

[11] s.6(5).
[12] s.3(5).
[13] s.33(2).
[14] s.6(6).
[15] Race Relations Act 1976, s.47(5). The same provision applies to the Equal
Opportunities Code.
[16] Immigration Act 1971, s.3(2).
[17] s.53(4).
[18] s.6 and Sched. 1.
[19] See *e.g.* Police & Criminal Evidence Bill, Standing Committee E, col. 1532
(March 1, 1984).
[20] 1979–1980; H.C. 822, para. 22—Report on Draft Codes on Picketing and the
Closed Shop and 1981–1982, H.C. 273, para. 18—Report on Draft Code on
Racial Discrimination and 1984–1985; H.C. 59—Report on the Equal
Opportunities Commission's Draft Code of Practice.
[21] These two points are by no means synonymous. By giving codes quasi-legal
effect they can extend the law; *supra*, p. 12.
[22] 1982–1983; H.C. 319.
[23] H.C. Deb., Vol. 40, col. 462 (March 31, 1983).

refusing his assent to the Code until the Commission revised it in accordance with the Employment Committee's recommendations.[24]

Where the Minister is himself responsible for preparing the code, a power of amendment can be achieved through the Green Paper procedure. This has been used for the Highway Code. When the revision of the Code was put before the House for approval in November 1968[25] there was much criticism of the procedure which did not allow the House of Commons to change the Code and the Government was refused the closure of the debate. During the adjourned debate, the Minister gave a pledge that on the next occasion the draft code would be circulated as a Green Paper before it was presented to the House for approval.[26] The next time was January 1975 when true to the earlier promise a Green Paper was published. A revised version was debated in the House of Commons on November 8, 1976 for two-and-a-half hours.[27] The Code was finally presented to the House for approval on November 24, 1977[28] after further amendment. This almost three-year long procedure amounted to overkill and led to the opposite cry for a shortened procedure. The Transport Act 1982,[29] therefore, now provides for a negative procedure except for alterations which are merely consequential on the passing of legislation. But, as was pointed out by Mr. Booth,[30] the affirmative resolution procedure, which requires a one-and-a-half-hour debate, can hardly be held responsible for the three-year delay. It is much more the result of the consultation procedure and this is not now required for merely consequential changes on the passing of new legislation. This should enable the Code to be kept up to date in between major revisions. It will be interesting to see if those will still involve a Green Paper procedure now that the Code is subject to annulment rather than approval.

When the Industrial Relations Act 1971 was being debated in the House, the Opposition tried unsuccessfully to introduce an amendment which would have made the Green Paper procedure obligatory for the Industrial Relations Code.[31] However, this

[24] 1982–1983; H.C. 319.
[25] H.C. Deb., Vol. 773, col. 1033 (November 18, 1968).
[26] H.C. Deb., Vol. 774, col. 1195 (December 2, 1968)—it was debated in the House of Lords on December 9, 1976—H.L. Deb., Vol. 378, col. 715.
[27] H.C. Deb., Vol. 919, col. 125.
[28] H.C. Deb., Vol. 939, col. 1915.
[29] s.60.
[30] Standing Committee F, col. 1153 (April 27, 1982).
[31] H.C. Deb., Vol. 814, col. 399 (March 23, 1971).

procedure was in fact followed, a Consultative Document on the code being debated in both Houses before an amended code was approved. In each case there was a full day's debate in the House of Commons.[32]

Even without a Green Paper procedure and even where the rules are only subject to a negative resolution, the House can achieve amendment by forcing the Minister to withdraw the rules and lay new ones before the House. This happened when the Immigration Rules were disapproved by the House in 1972[33] and the Government had to revise them before laying them a second time.[34] In 1982 the Government amended the proposals for revision of the Immigration Rules after a right-wing revolt on a take note debate.[35] They were then defeated on a resolution disapproving the amended rules[36] and finally succeeded by their being changed back towards their original form.[37]

These cases are, however, exceptional and underline the absence of a regular procedure for amendment of such rules by the House. It is hard to disagree with Mr. Bennett speaking about the proposed code of practice under the Police Bill 1983, "if [a Code of Practice] is to become a regular Government practice we must find a wholly new procedure for making introduction of the Code much more subject to parliamentary control so that there is an opportunity for amendment."[38] Exceptionally in that instance the draft code was available to the House when the Bill was being debated. This was not the case with the Industrial Relations Code or the codes under the Employment Act 1980.

In the latter case the Employment Committee was highly critical of the time-table adopted by the Secretary of State for consultation before a final draft was submitted to Parliament for approval. Most of this period fell into the summer recess and the Committee successfully asked the Secretary of State to postpone the laying of the codes until they had had time to take evidence.[39]

Select Committees. Consideration of codes of practice by the Departmental Select Committees appointed in 1979 has con-

---

[32] H.C. Deb., Vol. 823, col. 385 (October 19, 1971) and H.C. Deb., Vol. 830, col. 460 (February 2, 1972).
[33] H.C. Deb., Vol. 846, col. 1343 (November 22, 1972).
[34] H.C. Deb., Vol. 851, col. 577 (February 21, 1973).
[35] H.C. Deb., Vol. 31, col. 692 (November 11, 1982).
[36] H.C. Deb., Vol. 34, col. 355 (December 15, 1982).
[37] H.C. Deb., Vol. 37, col. 180 (February 15, 1983).
[38] Standing Committee J, col. 1042 (March 3, 1983).
[39] 1979–1980; H.C. 822, para. 6.

siderably enhanced parliamentary scrutiny and has done something to make up for the lack of an amending power. The Employment Committee was able to hear evidence from the Secretary of State and both sides of industry as well as the police and Mr. Enoch Powell, and to report to the House in time for the debate on the codes. Though the Secretary of State rejected most of their recommendations, which were not unanimous, he did make changes in the draft codes to clarify the distinction between explanation of the law and guidance in accordance with the Committee's recommendations. As we have seen, in the case of the Race Relations Code, the Commission was asked by the Secretary of State to revise the code in accordance with the Committee's recommendations. The Employment Committee took further evidence on the revised Race Relations Code[40] and on the revised Closed Shop Code[41] so that one member of the Committee complained that it was the fifth occasion in that Parliament when the Committee had been asked to look at a code and he thought that the practice was growing and ought to be diminished.[42] The later evidence did not lead to further reports.

Similarly, the Home Affairs Committee took evidence on revisions of the Immigration Rules before they were debated in the House but they failed to make any recommendations and merely set out the arguments adduced in evidence.[43] This was done to avoid the committee splitting along party lines as it could not have reached unanimous conclusions.[44] In the case of the revised Immigration Rules in 1982, it merely reported the evidence.[45]

The Welsh Affairs Committee has heard evidence and reported on draft guidelines to the Welsh Water Authority for the establishment of Local Consumer Advisory Committees. This was an interim report, produced separately and in advance of the main report on Water in Wales, so as to enable the

---

[40] 1982–1983; H.C. 213 iii.
[41] 1982–1983; H.C. 197 i and 1982–1983; H.C. 213 i.
[42] H.C. Deb., Vol. 40, col. 907 (April 13, 1983)—the Committee subsequently examined the Equal Opportunities Code 1984–1985; H.C. 59 and the Code of Good Practice on Employment of Disabled People (1984–1985; H.C. 32i.
[43] 1979–1980; H.C. 434, para. 20.
[44] Contrast the report of the Employment Committee, 1979–1980; H.C. 822.
[45] 1981–1982; H.C. 526.

Committees to be established quickly.[46] Some of their recommendations were accepted by the Government.[47]

The Departmental Committees, therefore, can perform a pre-legislative scrutiny in the case of codes of practice, rules, guidelines and circulars[48] when they are still at a formative stage and, though they cannot perform the function of a Standing Committee on a Bill, they can bring pressure to bear on the Minister to amend the instruments by a less cumbersome procedure than providing a Green Paper stage.

Another committee of the House, namely the Joint Select Committee on Statutory Instruments, performs a very different function. It can only look at documents which are not statutory instruments if they are subject to an affirmative resolution and only on grounds that do not impinge on the merits or policy. The Committee has looked at the revision of the Highway Code and drawn it to the attention of the House for technical reasons.[49] This Committee has also criticised subordinate legislation by Departmental circular, *e.g.* filling in details omitted from statutory instruments when the parent Act provides for the action to be taken by statutory instrument.[50]

The question of whether the Immigration Rules had been properly laid before the House when they were presented to the House as a Command Paper was taken to court and these terms were held to be synonymous.[51] In the case of the Race Relations Code which is subject to annulment within forty days, the period was interrupted by the General Election[52] so that it had to be completed after Parliament reassembled on June 15, 1983.

Where the code or rules are subject to Parliamentary procedure, the Government may, as we have seen, allow more than the one-and-a-half hours for a debate on an affirmative resolution or even a prayer where the subject is politically controversial, as in the case of the Industrial Relations and Employment

[46] 1981–1982; H.C. 335.
[47] 1981–1982; H.C. 499.
[48] The Environment Committee considered the Department's controversial draft circular on the Green Belt which had already been revised after much public pressure, 1983–1984; H.C. 275. As a result of the Committee's Report further revisions were made, H.C. Deb., Vol. 63, cols. 161–162, Written Answers, (July 4, 1984).
[49] 1977–1978; H.C. 16i.
[50] 1977–1978; H.L. 51.
[51] *R.* v. *Immigration Tribunal, ex p. Joyles* [1972] 1 W.L.R. 1390.
[52] Race Relations Act 1976, s.47(6), " . . . no account shall be taken of any period during which Parliament is dissolved . . . "

Codes, the Welfare of Livestock Codes in 1969[53] and the Immigration Rules. This is, however, exceptional and normally the debate would last one-and-a-half hours for an affirmative resolution whilst with a negative resolution the difficulty is to get it debated at all on the floor of the House within the time-limit. Only a prayer moved by a member of the Opposition Front Bench is guaranteed such a debate.[54] Even statutory codes are not always made subject to parliamentary procedure *e.g.* those made under the Health and Safety at Work Act 1974 and non-statutory ones such as tax concessions are by definition not subject to such a procedure. Where, however, the issue is highly controversial, the Government may submit its policy to Parliamentary approval to give it greater legitimacy. Thus the White Papers on Incomes Policy which provided for the "blacklist" of companies who broke the pay policy were approved by the House of Commons,[55] as was the policy on comprehensive education, later embodied in Circular 10/65, though in that case it was in the form of a Government amendment to an Opposition motion on a Supply Day.[56] The Fair Wages Resolution was, as its name implies, approved by the House of Commons,[57] as was its withdrawal by the Government in 1983.[58] Most dramatically of all the "blacklist" was withdrawn when the Government was defeated on this issue.[59]

Consultation and consensus

Since the use of consensus and persuasion rather than force are the main *raison d'être* of quasi-law, the consultation process leading up to their preparation is obviously crucial to their acceptability. The creation of consensus may be institutionalised by entrusting the preparation of the codes to a body composed of members representative of conflicting interests. Thus the codes under the Health and Safety at Work Act 1974, s.16 have to be approved by the Health and Safety Commission, which has

[53] H.C. Deb., Vol. 788, col. 825 (October 20, 1969).
[54] H.C. Deb., Vol. 41, col. 969 (April 25, 1983). Only statutory instruments and draft statutory instruments can be considered in a Standing Committee on Statutory Instruments; see S.O. 79.
[55] See Ganz [1978] P.L. 334, n. 4.
[56] H.C. Deb., Vol. 705, col. 415 (January 21, 1965). Similarly there was an adjournment debate on the Green Belt circular, H.C. Deb., Vol. 48, col. 1156 (November 18, 1983).
[57] H.C. Deb., Vol. 427, col. 619 (October 14, 1946).
[58] H.C. Deb., Vol. 34, col. 499 (December 16, 1983).
[59] H.C. Deb., Vol. 960, col. 673 *et seq.* (December 13, 1978) and H.C. Deb., Vol. 960, col. 920 *et seq.* (December 14, 1978).

members from both sides of industry.[60] Similarly, the Race Relations Act 1976, s.47 gives the responsibility for issuing codes of practice to the Commission for Racial Equality which includes two members from each side of industry.[61] In each case the consent of the Secretary of State is also necessary and there are provisions for consultations with appropriate bodies.[62] In the case of Health and Safety at Work Codes, we have seen that it was the need for consultations which has been largely responsible for the delay in producing codes. "The full participation of all concerned with the hazard is essential, however, if proposals are to be realistic and to gain acceptance."[63] The Commission itself has to reach decisions by consensus because once a solution has been agreed those whom it represents have been committed to that solution and have to stick by it. Differences have to be resolved through continuous and persistent discussions until agreement is reached.[64]

Similarly, the Race Relations Commission operates by consensus. The four Commissioners, drawn from both sides of industry, agreed on the need for a code and the provisions in it.[65] The Commission started informal discussions in 1979 with both sides of industry, A.C.A.S., the Department of Employment and ethnic minority groups and race-relations bodies. Formal consultations were then held before a consultative draft code was published in 1980 which led to representations from a wide range of bodies after which a revised draft was drawn up and submitted to the Secretary of State.[66] As we have seen, this was further revised by the Commission in line with the recommendations of the Employment Committee before it was approved by the Secretary of State and laid before the House in March 1983. It was not to come into force until April 1984 to allow employers and others reasonable time to consider the Code and

[60] s.10.
[61] 1981–1982; H.C. 273, para. 12.
[62] 1974 Act, s.16(2); 1976 Act, s.47(3) and s.47(4). s.47(2) also provides that the Commission shall prepare and publish a draft code and consider any representations about the draft and modify the draft accordingly.
[63] 1981–1982; H.C. 400, para. 10.
[64] *Ibid.* Evidence p. 74.
[65] 1981–1982; H.C. 273, para. 12.
[66] *Ibid.* para. 5.

its implications for them.[67] Thus it has taken five years to acclimatise industry to the Code.[68]

In the case of the Welfare of Livestock Codes, though the Minister is given the responsibility for their preparation after consultation with those appearing to him to represent the interests concerned,[69] the codes were in fact drawn up by the Farm Animal Welfare Advisory Committee, whose members spanned the conflicting interests including scientists, persons interested in animal welfare, farmers and veterinarians. They visited intensive farming establishments and obtained much first-hand evidence on factory farming before drawing up the codes which were then circulated widely among interested organisations. Their comments, supplemented by oral representations, were taken into account before the codes were presented to the Minister, who accepted them *in toto*.[70] But in this case, unlike the Health and Safety and Race Relations Codes, there was no consensus on the Drafting Committee. Three members thought there should be further consideration before the codes were approved and they were publicly criticised by the animal welfare organisations. However, the Government thought it was better to go ahead than start again from scratch and pointed to the provision for revision of the codes which has happened on several occasions.

The problem of obtaining consensus in the preparation of codes of practice has been most acute in the realm of industrial relations. So far as codes under the Employment Act 1975 are concerned, consensus has been institutionalised by giving responsibility for the codes to A.C.A.S. subject to approval of the Secretary of State.[71] A.C.A.S. consists of representatives from both sides of industry as well as independent members. It is obliged to prepare the draft codes and consider representations made about them. The crucial difference from codes under the Industrial Relations Act 1971 and the Employment Act 1980 is that these are entrusted to the Secretary of State. Under the 1971 Act, which was substantially re-enacted in 1974, he must consult

---

[67] 1982–1983; H.C. 319.

[68] See 1983–1984; H.C. 556i, App. I—Evidence to the Employment Committee—for the elaborate consultation undertaken by the Equal Opportunities Commission in respect of their code of practice. The code is the result of nearly ten years' experience monitoring the Sex Discrimination Act 1975.

[69] Agriculture (Miscellaneous Provisions) Act 1968, s.3(1).

[70] H.C. Deb., Vol. 788, col. 827 *et seq.* (October 20, 1969). The Farm Animal Welfare Advisory Committee was criticised and compared unfavourably to its successor in evidence to the Agriculture Committee, 1980–1981; H.C. 406, Q.4.

[71] s.6.

the T.U.C. and C.B.I. on revisions of the code,[72] whilst the 1980 Act provides for consultation with A.C.A.S. and the consideration of any representations made about a draft code.[73] In 1971 the T.U.C. was strongly opposed to the Industrial Relations Code and did not join in consultations but issued its own code, which was substantially different. In 1980 A.C.A.S. refused to comment on the draft codes on Picketing and the Closed Shop because they wished to maintain their impartiality. As we have seen, the Employment Committee commented adversely on the consultation period falling during the summer recess. The T.U.C. had drawn up their own code on picketing in 1979. They were totally opposed to both codes. When consulted about the revised code on closed shop agreements they replied, "We consider that the provisions of the draft code are as irrelevant to the promotion of good industrial relations as all the other legislative steps taken by you (and your predecessor) since the Government took office in 1979."[74] During the debate on the 1980 Codes[75] they were compared unfavourably, not only by Opposition M.P.s, to the A.C.A.S. Codes[76] which were the result of agreement between both sides of industry and not rejected by either side as the T.U.C. utterly rejected the 1980 Codes. The Secretary of State took comfort from the fact that the Industrial Relations Code 1972 had also been rejected by the T.U.C. but was largely kept in being by the Act of 1974. It is doubtful whether this precedent is on all fours, as the main objection to the 1972 Code was its guilt by association with the 1971 Act rather than the Code as such. The objections of the T.U.C. to the 1980 Codes are much more fundamental—they are seen as part of the continued attempts to weaken effective trade unionism.

Apart from the above cases there are numerous other examples of statutory provisions providing for consultation "with such bodies as appear to the Minister to be concerned"[77] and to consider representations.[78] In the case of the Wildlife and Countryside Act 1981, s.33(1) also provides for consultation of

[72] Trade Union and Labour Relations Act 1974, s.2(1), Sched. 1.
[73] s.3.
[74] 1982–1983; H.C. 197i, p. 9.
[75] H.C. Deb., Vol. 992, col. 676 (November 13, 1980).
[76] Three Codes have been issued—
    1. Disciplinary practice and procedure in employment.
    2. Disclosure of information.
    3. Time off for trade union duties and activities.
[77] *e.g.* Mental Health (Amendment) Act 1982, s.53(3).
[78] *e.g.* Police and Criminal Evidence Act 1984, s.67.

the Nature Conservancy Council. The Minister in addition consulted the National Farmers' Union and the Country Landowners' Association and then held a public consultation with 150 organisations.[79] As we saw, there was very extensive consultation on the 1977 revision of the Highway Code, which was published as a Green Paper but the duty of the Minister to consult "such representative organisations as he thinks fit" was not embodied in legislation till the Transport Act 1982, s.60. Similarly the codes under the Control of Pollution Act 1974 were prepared following consultation with a wide range of interested bodies[80] even though there are no statutory provisions about consultation. The convention about consultation in respect of delegated legislation which has spread to quasi-legislation, whether made under statutory provisions or extra-statutory,[81] is so well-established that its embodiment in legislation is more of symbolic than practical importance.

Publication

Since knowledge of quasi-law is just as vital as knowledge of the law, publication is of fundamental importance. It would be impossible to devise a more bizarre and haphazard system than that which has grown up from a maze of individual provisions with very little attempt at consistency or systematisation.

If the rule is in the form of a statutory instrument, as was the case under the Counter-Inflation Act 1973, the provisions of the Statutory Instruments Act 1946 apply to printing and to publication. *Blackpool Corporation* v. *Locker*[82] illustrates the problem where a circular was held to contain sub-delegated legislation but not to fall under the Statutory Instruments Act and did not therefore have to be published. On the other hand in *Scott* v. *Baker*[83] the court refused to accept a circular which had not been published as evidence of approval by the Minister of the *Alcotest* breath test device. It was not until the approval was contained in an Order made by the Minister and published by H.M.S.O. that the court in *R.* v. *Clarke*[84] allowed it to be proved by production of a copy printed by H.M.S.O. in accordance with Section 2 of the Documentary Evidence Act 1868. The court

[79] H.C. Deb., Vol. 29, col. 301 (October 19, 1982).
[80] D.O.E. Circular 2/82.
[81] *e.g.* D.O.E. Circular on Green Belts, see H.C. Deb., Vol. 48, col. 1154 *et seq.* (November 18, 1983).
[82] [1948] 1 K.B. 349.
[83] [1968] 3 W.L.R. 796.
[84] [1969] 2 W.L.R. 505.

held that, "the word 'order' in the Act should be given a wide meaning covering at any rate any executive act of government performed by the bringing into existence of a public document for the purpose of giving effect to an Act of Parliament."[85] This would cover many of the instruments in which quasi-law is embodied, though, as we shall see, the methods of publication are very diverse.

The most explicit provision for publication exists for the Highway Code—"The Secretary of State shall cause the Highway Code to be printed and may cause copies of it to be sold to the public at such price as he may determine."[86] The Code is published and sold by H.M.S.O. but is also distributed free to those obtaining a driving licence for the first time. An identical provision was made in the case of the Code for areas of special scientific interest under the Wildlife and Countryside Act 1981, s.33(3) and the Welfare of Livestock Codes under the Agriculture (Miscellaneous Provisions) Act 1968, s.3(3). But whereas the code under the Wildlife Act is published by H.M.S.O., the Livestock Codes are published by the Ministry of Agriculture and must be obtained from there, though they have been distributed free to livestock keepers, veterinary surgeons and agricultural education centres. Strangely enough when the Industrial Relations Act 1971 was in its Committee stage in the House of Commons, the Government deleted an identical provision on the ground that selling and pricing were a matter for H.M.S.O. and not the Minister.[87] The Act merely provided that the Secretary of State shall issue the code once it had been approved by Parliament.[88] It was published by H.M.S.O.

Some Acts provide for the preparation and publishing of draft codes to enable representations to be made. In the case of the Employment Acts 1975[89] and 1980[90] the draft codes were published as Consultative Documents which were not published by H.M.S.O. and the same procedure was followed in the case of the draft Race Relations Code. On the other hand draft codes of practice under the Health and Safety at Work Act 1974, which provides for consultation with appropriate bodies[91] but does not

---

[85] p. 509 H.
[86] See now Road Traffic Act 1972, s.37(6).
[87] H.C. Deb., Vol. 810, col. 560 (January 27, 1971).
[88] s.3(2).
[89] A.C.A.S., Annual Reports 1976 and 1977.
[90] Department of Employment.
[91] s.16(2).

require publication of draft codes, have been published by H.M.S.O.

There is similarly no consistency about publication of the final code where the Act provides that the code shall be issued. Codes under the Industrial Relations Act 1971, the Employment Act 1975, the Control of Pollution Act 1974 and the Health and Safety at Work Act 1974 as well as the Equal Opportunities Code are published by H.M.S.O., whereas the Race Relations Code is not and the codes under the Employment Act 1980 are published by the Department of Employment. This is not just a technicality as H.M.S.O. publications can be easily purchased whereas non-H.M.S.O. publications must be obtained from the Department or other body and otherwise are only easily accessible if they are available in the Catalogue of British Official Publications published by Chadwyck-Healey, a private enterprise undertaking.

The codes of practice relating to the publication of information by local authorities which may be issued under the Local Government, Planning and Land Act 1980, s.2 have either been contained in Department of the Environment circulars published by H.M.S.O. or have been published separately by H.M.S.O. Recent legislation adding further recruits to the growing army of codes of practice provides that "The Secretary of State shall publish the code as for the time being in force."[92] The Immigration Rules fall into a special category of their own. The Immigration Appeals Act 1969, s.24(2) provided that immigration rules means rules which have been published and laid before Parliament. They were presented to Parliament in the form of Command Papers. The Immigration Act 1971, s.3(2) provided for the laying before Parliament of a statement of the rules and made them subject to annulment. The rules are now in the form of House of Commons Papers and are, therefore, published as such.

Where an Act provides for the making of quasi-law but makes no provision for publication, there is even more scope for variety. Thus the code of guidance under the Housing (Homeless Persons) Act 1977, s.12, which provided for the Minister to give guidance to local authorities to which they must have regard, was published by H.M.S.O.,[93] as was the guidance for payments

---

[92] Mental Health (Amendment) Act 1982, s.53(6). Health and Social Services and Social Security Adjudications Act 1983, s.6 and Sched. 1. The latter code is contained in D.H.S.S. circular L.A.C. (83) 19.

[93] The earlier non-statutory guidance was contained in D.O.E. and D.H.S.S. circular 18/74—also published by H.M.S.O.

in connection with management agreements under the Wildlife and Countryside Act 1981, s.50(2), though this was also published in a D.O.E. circular.[94] Guidance under the Police Act 1976, s.3(8) to the Police Complaints Board by the Home Secretary, to which the Board had to have regard, seems to have been contained in a letter, according to McNeill J. in the *Madden* v. *Rhone* case, although he saw no copy of it.[95] This guidance referred in its turn to non-statutory guidance by the Home Secretary to Chief Constables which was contained in a Home Office circular.[96] Whilst most D.O.E. circulars of interest to the public are published by H.M.S.O.,[97] only some Home Office circulars are published and then only by the Department.

Circulars are very frequently used for non-statutory guidance, especially to local authorities, the most famous examples being the circulars which promulgated the Government's policy on comprehensive education. Circulars from the Department of Education are also published by H.M.S.O. But circulars are only one mechanism for conveying non-statutory guidance.

The extra-statutory tax concessions granted by the Inland Revenue were published for the first time as an Appendix to the Annual Report of the Commissioners of Inland Revenue in 1950.[98] These were added to in later reports and since 1966 they were published as a separate booklet by the Inland Revenue but not H.M.S.O. But these are only the concessions which apply generally, not those which affect particular individuals.

The Criminal Injuries Compensation Scheme was set up in 1964 through the medium of a White Paper.[99] It was amended by Ministerial statements in the House of Commons in the form of Written Answers and the latest revised scheme is set out in full in a Written Answer.[1] The Criminal Injuries Compensation

[94] 4/83.

[95] [1983] 1 W.L.R. 447, 453 B.

[96] The guidance to Chief Constables has now been put on a statutory basis by the Police and Criminal Evidence Act, s.105. Revised guidance in 1983 was contained in Cmnd. 9072.

[97] There are also unpublished circulars sent direct to local authorities and messages which the local authority associations are asked to pass on to their members. Some of the latter sent since May 1, 1979 were listed in H.C. Deb., Vol. 979, col. 551, Written Answers (February 26, 1980).

[98] Cmd. 8103 (1950) and see Williams [1979] B.T.R. 137. The booklet also excludes concessions which apply only in special and narrow circumstances and these are made known to the category of people affected by them. Customs and Excise do not publish a list of class concessions, see 1981–1982; H.C. 339, para. 34.

[99] Cmnd. 2323.

[1] H.C. Deb., Vol. 971, col. 17 *et seq.*, Written Answers (July 23, 1979).

Board, which administers the scheme, has published its interpretation of the scheme as an Annex to its Annual Report.[2]

It is revealing to contrast publicity for this scheme with the way in which the Government published the pay policy and its interpretation which was crucial for determining whether a firm would be blacklisted for breach of the policy. The counter-inflation policy was published as a White Paper, which also set out the policy on sanctions for its breach. But the detailed interpretation of the White Paper for use by civil servants did not see the light of day till it was published by *The Times*[3]. The Government are not always so secretive. They will often publish guidance on the administration of schemes[4] but sometimes such documents would not be published if they were not demanded by Select Committees. A good example is the document *Criteria for Assistance to Industry* about which a parliamentary question was asked.[5] It was then placed in the library of the House of Commons,[6] but it was first published by the Expenditure Committee.[7] Similarly the famous, or perhaps infamous, *Memorandum of Guidance for Officials appearing before Select Committees* was revealed to the Select Committee on Procedure with great reluctance.[8] The most notorious example of secret guidelines on the exercise of discretion was the "A" Code under which supplementary benefit was administered by Supplementary Benefit Officers before the scheme was recast in 1980.[9] Standing orders and circular instructions under the Prison Rules have also not been published but standing orders have been placed in the libraries of both Houses of Parliament. Since December 1981 the standing order dealing with prisoners' correspondence has been published and made available to prisoners.[10] If Britain had a Freedom of Information Act[11] or even a code of practice[12] for the disclosure of departmental documents, such guidance would be obtainable as of right.

It is difficult to imagine a more haphazard system for

---

[2] *e.g.* Cmnd. 7022, Annex F.

[3] *The Times*, September 29, 1978.

[4] *e.g.* Regional Development Grants, see Ganz, *Government and Industry*, p. 41, and guidelines for grants under s.7, Industry Act 1972, *ibid.* p. 22.

[5] H.C. Deb., Vol. 902, col. 894, Written Answers (December 19, 1975).

[6] H.C. Deb., Vol. 903, col. 7, Written Answers (January 12, 1976).

[7] 1975–1976; H.C. 596–II, p. 113.

[8] 1977–1978; H.C. 588–I, para. 7.12 and Appendix D.

[9] Social Security Act 1980.

[10] *Halsbury's Laws of England* (4th Edition), vol. 37, para. 1103.

[11] See *e.g.* the abortive Freedom of Information Bill 1981, cl. 13.

[12] As recommended by Justice, *Freedom of Information* (1978).

publishing or not publishing rules which may have legal force directly or indirectly or interpret legal provisions or structure the exercise of official discretion. It should at least be possible to make statutory provisions for publication more consistent and then to implement them uniformly by using H.M.S.O. for publication. Where there are no statutory provisions it would also be possible to develop conventions about the use of White Papers, circulars, annual reports and Written Answers. But more importantly there ought to be conventions about what guidance should be published. As Justice recommended, there should be a presumption in favour of publication unless such documents fall within certain limited exceptions.

Control over Interpretation and Application

So far we have been concerned with control over the making and the publication of quasi-legal rules. We must now turn to controls over their interpretation and application.

Judicial control. Where a code can be relied on in legal proceedings as is the case, for example, with the Highway Code, the Health and Safety Codes, the Welfare of Livestock Codes, the Control of Noise Codes, and the codes under the Employment Act 1980 and the Police and Criminal Evidence Act 1984, their construction and interpretation is a matter directly for the courts. Where, on the other hand, the code is admissible in evidence only before tribunals, such as the Race Relations Code, the A.C.A.S. codes and the Industrial Relations Code, they will be interpreted in the first instance by the relevant tribunal. The A.C.A.S. codes are also admissible in evidence before the Central Arbitration Committee.[13] This is also the body which determined whether the Fair Wages Resolution had been breached,[14] an independent method of arbitration which was never conceded for the companies blacklisted for breach of the Government's pay policy.[15] Interpretation may on the other hand be entrusted to a quasi-governmental body such as the Price Commission which interpreted the Price Code under the Counter-Inflation Act 1973. Such an interpretation is then subject to the supervisory jurisdiction of the courts.

[13] Employment Act 1975, s.6(11).
[14] A test case was brought by the National Union of Public Employees against a private refuse collecting firm employed by Wandsworth B.C., *The Guardian*, May 17, 1983.
[15] Ganz [1978] P.L. 333, 341.

The normal principles of judicial control apply and these were reiterated in two cases against the Price Commission, *G.E.C.* v. *Price Commission*[16] and *H.T.V. Ltd.* v. *Price Commission*.[17] So far as interpretation is concerned Lord Denning M.R. said, "The courts will ensure that the body acts in accordance with the law. If a question arises on the interpretation of words, the courts will decide it by declaring what is the correct interpretation."[18] And Scarman L.J. (as he then was) put it thus,

> "Undoubtedly questions of fact and policy arising in the course of implementing the Code are for the Commission, not the courts. But the interpretation of statutory language (including the language of delegated legislation) is a matter of law.... Applying these general principles, I have no doubt that it is for the courts to determine the meaning of paragraph 39...."[19]

This approach contrasts with that adopted by Lord Roskill *vis-à-vis* the Immigration Rules in *R.* v. *Immigration Appeal Tribunal, ex p. Alexander*[20] where he said,

> "These rules are not to be construed with all the strictness applicable to the construction of a Statute or a Statutory Instrument.[21] They must be construed sensibly according to the natural meaning of the language which is employed. The rules give guidance to the various officers concerned and contain statements of general policy regarding the operation of the relevant immigration legislation."

The courts have even exercised their supervisory jurisdiction over the Criminal Injuries Compensation Board, though it is a non-statutory body administering a scheme of *ex gratia* compensation which is not legally enforceable.[22] In a subsequent case Bridge J. (as he then was) seemed aware of this anomaly when he said in a dissenting judgment,

> "Accepting that [*ex p. Lain*], as I am bound to do, I still think one must bear in mind that the scheme, as the

---

[16] [1975] I.C.R. 1.
[17] [1976] I.C.R. 170.
[18] [1975] I.C.R. 1, 12.
[19] [1976] I.C.R. 170, 188–189.
[20] [1982] 1 W.L.R. 1076, 1080 G.
[21] But, as we have seen, this affects the form not the force of the rule.
[22] *R.* v. *Criminal Injuries Compensation Board, ex p. Lain* [1967] 3 W.L.R. 348—a landmark case, see *C.C.S.U.* v. *Minister for Civil Service* [1984] 3 W.L.R. 1174, 1194D and 1203H, *per* Lords Scarman and Roskill.

document is entitled which enshrines the rules for the board's conduct, is not recognisable as any kind of legislative document with which the court is familiar. It is not expressed in the kind of language one expects from a parliamentary draftsman, whether of statutes or statutory instruments. It bears all the hallmarks of a document which lays down the broad guidelines of policy... against that background it seems to me that it would be wrong for this court to intervene and say that the board have misconstrued the scheme unless it is very clear that that is the only tenable view."[23]

This approach did not commend itself to his fellow judges who reached a different conclusion in their interpretation of the scheme.

The approach did, however, commend itself to the Court of Appeal in *R.* v. *Criminal Injuries Board, ex p. Thompstone*[24] where Sir John Donaldson M.R. said, "The scheme is discretionary and the discretion is that of the board. It follows that the board's decisions can be reviewed if it misconstrues its mandate or, on *Wednesbury* principles must be deemed to have done so since its decision is one which no reasonable body could have reached on the facts if it had correctly construed its mandate." A broad non-legalistic interpretation was also said to be the right approach to planning circulars in *Mid-Bedfordshire District Council* v. *Secretary of State for the Environment*[25] by McCullough J. He said, "These circulars were intended to provide local authorities with general guidance. Their paragraphs are to be read with common sense. Words are to be given their ordinary meaning and the sense and purpose of a paragraph as a whole, and indeed of a circular as a whole, is of greater importance than any individual phrase, or sentence contained in it." There are thus two approaches to the interpretation of quasi-legislation, one of strict statutory construction and the broad common sense approach. Whether the court substitutes its judgement on the interpretation of the document will depend on which of these approaches it chooses to adopt and this may depend on whether it is in the form of a statutory instrument or a less formal document.

Logically prior to interpretation is the determination whether such guidance whether statutory or not is lawful. Parallel with

---

[23] *R.* v. *Criminal Injuries Board, ex p. Schofield* [1971] 1 W.L.R. 926, 931D.
[24] [1984] 1 W.L.R. 1234, 1238H. See also *R.* v. *Criminal Injuries Board ex p. Webb* [1986] 3 W.L.R. 251, 254B.
[25] Unreported decision, see [1984] J.P.L. 623, 631.

the growth of quasi-legislation there has been an increasing
number of cases where its legality has been challenged for a
variety of reasons. In a *cause célèbre*, the Court of Appeal in
Laker Airways Ltd. v. *Department of Trade*[26] held that guidance
given by the Secretary of State under the Civil Aviation Act 1971
to the Civil Aviation Authority was *ultra vires* the Act. In a less
celebrated decision *R.* v. *Waveney District Council, ex p.
Bowers*[27] the Court of Appeal held that the Council had placed
too much reliance on the code of guidance under the Housing
(Homeless Persons) Act 1977 which led them to the conclusion
that accommodation had to be provided only for those in
substantial need, whereas the first question which had to be
considered under the Act was vulnerability and whether it arose
as a result of old age, mental illness or handicap or physical
disability or other special reason. The decision underlines the
legal position that, where a code is interpreting an Act, it is the
Act which is binding not the code. The same applies to purely
non-statutory guidance, such as planning circulars which have
been held to misinterpret statutory provisions.[28] A planning
circular has also been held to be *ultra vires* because it laid down a
procedure which fettered the discretion of the local planning
authority.[29] Again part of a local development plan was quashed
by the House of Lords because it left some of the policies to be
formulated by non-statutory guidance rather than in the plan
itself. This was held to be in breach of the local authority's
statutory duties under the Town and Country Planning Act
1971.[30]

The most spectacular challenge to a departmental circular was
undoubtedly made by Mrs. Gillick.[31] She asked that a Health
Service circular which outlined the arrangements for a family
planning service within the National Health Service and which
was accompanied by a memorandum of guidance which contained *inter alia* guidelines about contraceptive treatment and

[26] [1977] 2 W.L.R. 234; for criticism see Baldwin, [1978] P.L. 57.
[27] [1982] 3 W.L.R. 661. Conversely in *Re M.* [1985] 2 W.L.R. 811 a statutory
code was used as an aid to construction of the section under which it was
made, which seems to put the cart before the horse.
[28] See cases cited in [1984] J.P.L. 623, 626.
[29] *R.* v. *Worthing Borough Council, The Times,* November 22, 1983. In *R.* v.
Home Secretary, ex p. Anderson [1984] 2 W.L.R. 725 a prison standing order
was held *ultra vires* as impeding the prisoner's access to the courts.
[30] *Westminster City Council* v. *Great Portland Estates P.L.C.* [1984] 3 W.L.R.
1035.
[31] *Gillick* v. *West Norfolk and Wisbech Area Health Authority* [1983] 3 W.L.R.
859, [1985] 2 W.L.R. 413 (C.A.); [1985] 3 W.L.R. 830 (H.L.).

advice to girls under 16 should be declared unlawful. Woolf J., who refused the declaration on substantive grounds, justified the propriety of the remedy thus,

> "In issuing the guidance the department were exercising their statutory functions and, if in the course of doing so, they were giving advice which was unlawful, or more accurately, if the advice, if followed, would result in unlawful acts, then their decision to do so could be challenged on the conventional ground that it was wholly unreasonable to exercise their discretion to give advice with this result."[32]

He then drew the analogy with *Royal College of Nursing of the United Kingdom* v. *Department of Health and Social Security*[33] where a declaration was granted to the Royal College that a departmental circular setting out procedures for carrying out abortions was unlawful. In the Court of Appeal it was conceded that if Mrs. Gillick could establish her case it followed that the department's notice was contrary to law and must be struck down under the *Wednesbury* principles.[34] The novelty of the case lies in applying the *Wednesbury* principles not to a Minister's decision based on an erroneous circular but to the making of the circular itself. In the House of Lords[35] where the decision of the Court of Appeal was reversed by 3:2, only Lord Bridge, one of the majority, and Lord Templeman, one of the dissenters, dealt with this issue. Lord Bridge thought that the circular which had no statutory force and was purely advisory could not be challenged on *Wednesbury* principles and that as a general rule such non-statutory guidance was not subject to judicial review. He concluded, however, that the *Royal College of Nursing* case had extended judicial review.

> "We must now say that if a government department in a field of administration in which it exercises responsibility, promulgates in a public document, albeit non-statutory in form, advice which is erroneous in law, then the court, in proceedings in appropriate form commenced by an applicant or plaintiff who possesses the necessary *locus standi*,

---

[32] [1983] 3 W.L.R. 859, 865G.
[33] [1981] 2 W.L.R. 279.
[34] [1985] 2 W.L.R. 413, 420A.
[35] [1985] 3 W.L.R. 830.

has jurisdiction to correct the error of law by an appropriate declaration."[36]

But he thought that such jurisdiction should be exercised with the utmost restraint where questions of social and ethical controversy were interwoven with the legal issues. Lord Templeman accepted this *caveat* but held that the questions raised had to be answered. He said, "The issue is not whether the D.H.S.S. are exercising a statutory discretion in a reasonable way but whether by mistake of law the D.H.S.S., a public authority, purports by the memorandum to authorise and approve an unlawful interference with parental rights."[37]

A similar assault on a Minister's policy directly by asking the court to declare it unlawful was made in *Re Findlay*.[38] The Home Secretary had announced changes in the policy in accordance with which he proposed to exercise his discretion to grant parole to certain serious offenders. The policy was attacked mainly on the ground that it fettered the Minister's discretion. The challenge failed on the well-established principle[39] that the policy would be departed from in exceptional circumstances or for compelling reasons. Though direct challenge of a policy is not unknown,[40] more commonly a circular or policy will be challenged indirectly by attacking the decision which has applied it. Success will depend on the legality or otherwise of the instrument and on whether the court thinks it has been applied correctly. By the application of the *Wednesbury* principles the courts can not only give legal effect to purely non-statutory guidelines,[41] but conversely they can have an invalidating effect. In *Gillick* they were used to invalidate the guidelines themselves. But this was disapproved in the House of Lords by two of their Lordships who did, however, hold that the guidance was open to judicial review for error of law. The parallel with *Lain* is close.

Parliamentary Commissioner for Administration. The P.C.A. can monitor the application of extra-statutory guidance within the context of maladministration. Firstly he can question the rules themselves to the extent of asking the Department to reconsider

---

[36] p. 862G-H.
[37] p. 874F-G.
[38] [1984] 3 W.L.R. 1159.
[39] *British Oxygen Ltd.* v. *Board of Trade* [1971] A.C. 610.
[40] *Att.-Gen., ex rel. Tilley* v. *Wandsworth L.B.C.* [1981] 1 W.L.R. 854; *R.* v. *Metropolitan Police Commissioner, ex p. Blackburn* [1968] 2 W.L.R. 893.
[41] *Supra,* p. 16.

the rules if they fall into the category of "bad rules" *i.e.* where their correct application causes hardship. But if the Department decide to adhere to the rules he is *functus officio* though the Select Committee on the P.C.A. can go further and comment on the merit of the rules.

He can also recommend redress where a complainant has been misled by the Department and this can include cases where the rules have been changed or the interpretation modified and applicants have relied on the old policy to their detriment. This is analogous to the estoppel rule and the P.C.A. dealt with a number of such cases when investment grants were first introduced in 1966.[42] Though the P.C.A. firmly refused to act as a Court of Appeal from the Department in such cases, he does sometimes come close to performing such a function in determining whether the rules have been applied properly. In his first *cause célèbre*, the *Sachsenhausen* case,[43] he came close to saying that the administrative rules, the "Butler Rules" in accordance with which compensation was paid to former prisoners of war, had been incorrectly applied. He was asked in one case to rule on the interpretation of the Government's 1975 White Paper, *The Attack on Inflation*.[44] He rejected the complaint but he investigated whether the Department had considered all the facts and applied the guidelines consistently with other cases. Though the P.C.A. could not have entertained a complaint from a blacklisted company because contractual and commercial transactions are outside his terms of reference,[45] the Select Committee on the P.C.A. recommended that this paragraph should be deleted.[46] They thought that this would not have enabled him to question the policy of blacklisting companies, because he cannot question the merits of a decision taken without maladministration,[47] but they thought that he should be able to investigate complaints that such a policy was not being applied uniformly or equitably.

The P.C.A. can investigate the application of extra-statutory tax concessions on a similar basis—*i.e.* he cannot act as a court of appeal from the Inland Revenue but he could see that the concessions are interpreted consistently and equitably.[48] The

[42] Ganz, *Government and Industry*, p. 35 *et seq.*
[43] 1967–1968; H.C. 54.
[44] 1976–1977; H.C. 223, p. 21, Case No. C225/K.
[45] Parliamentary Commissioner Act 1967, Sched. 3, para. 9.
[46] 1977–1978; H.C. 615, para. 24.
[47] s.12(3).
[48] *cf.* Williams [1979] B.T.R. 137, 144.

equitable jurisdiction of the P.C.A. is well illustrated by a case involving a concession where the Revenue acted in accordance with a published concession but as a result of the P.C.A.'s reference to them of the complaint, the Inland Revenue decided to extend the scope of the concession to cover the complainant and others in similar circumstances.[49]

The Public Accounts Committee and other Select Committees. Extra-statutory concessions are also very much the concern of the Public Accounts Committee. They have approved arrangements whereby any new extra-statutory concessions, or modifications to existing ones, affecting classes and schedules of amounts remitted or written off for individual taxpayers have to be furnished annually to the Comptroller and Auditor General who can bring them to notice in his Report to the Public Accounts Committee.[50] The Committee has been concerned to eliminate or reduce class concessions by having them embodied in statute[51] but it has also asked questions about their application. It has wanted to be assured that the concessions were publicly known and were applied uniformly and without fear or favour.[52] This is particularly important as the rubric relating to concessions in the Annual Report of the Commissioners reads, "The concessions described within are of general application but it must be borne in mind that in a particular case there may be special circumstances which will require to be taken into account in considering the application of the concession."[53] As Du Parcq L.J. said, " . . . it exposes revenue officials to temptation, which is wrong, even in the case of a service like the Inland Revenue, characterised by a wonderfully high sense of honour."[54] Other Select Committees may also monitor the operation of codes of practice, though usually in the wider context of policy. Thus the Employment Committee were concerned with codes of practice in their Report on the Working of the Health and Safety

---

[49] 1970–1971; H.C. 261, p. 158, Case No. C 172/S. In the case of remission of arrears of tax resulting from error of the Inland Revenue on the basis of hardship, the rules themselves were drawn up by the Government in response to the prompting of the Select Committee on the P.C.A. (Cmnd. 4729 (1971). The Public Accounts Committee were not ecstatic about the recommendation. 1970–1971; H.C. 300–I, Q.3371, *et seq.* The P.C.A. deals with complaints against the application of the White Paper in accordance with his normal rules.

[50] 1981–1982; H.C. 339, para. 29 *et seq.*

[51] *Ibid.*

[52] 1968–1969; H.C. 185 I, Q.3011–Q3019. The C. & A.G. can report any questionable use of the dispensing power.

[53] Cmnd. 8103 (1980), Annex.

[54] *Absalom* v. *Talbot* [1943] 1 All E.R. 589, 598A.

Commission[55] and the Agriculture Committee looked at the function of codes in their Report on Animal Welfare.[56] Again the Environment Committee in their Report on the Wildlife and Countryside Act 1981[57] endorsed the voluntary approach embodied in the codes of practice.

Parliamentary questions. Select Committees do not normally concern themselves with individual cases but these can be raised with M.P.s who then have the usual parliamentary procedures available to them. Parliamentary questions have been asked about concessions[58] as well as about codes of practice such as the Welfare of Livestock Codes,[59] in particular about cases where the codes have not been observed.

Council on Tribunals. Where the codes of practice are procedural ones, *e.g.* the codes of practice on informal planning appeal hearings, major public inquiries and examinations in public, as well as the other non-statutory procedural rules contained in circulars, they fall within the jurisdiction of the Council on Tribunals who will not only be consulted at the drafting stage but will also monitor them and entertain complaints that they have not been observed.[60] The code of practice on the publication of information about the handling of planning applications made under the Local Government, Planning and Land Act 1980 will be monitored by the Local Authority Associations who should ensure that their members comply with the code.[61]

Consumer codes. The Director of Fair Trading is charged with the duty of encouraging trade associations to prepare codes of practice to promote the interests of consumers. As a corollary of this duty he is also concerned with the monitoring of these codes.[62] In the case of the nationalised industries this task is shared with the Consumer Councils.[63] The Gas and Electricity Consumer Councils are also charged with monitoring the Code of Practice on fuel bills and disconnections.[64] So far as British

---

[55] 1981–1982; H.C. 400.   [56] 1980–1981; H.C. 406.
[57] 1984–1985; H.C. 6.
[58] See Williams, [1979] B.T.R. 137, n. 4.
[59] *e.g.* H.C. Deb., Vol. 830, col. 1124 (February 8, 1972).
[60] Council on Tribunals, Annual Report (1981–1982), paras. 2.16, 4.9 and 4.10.
[61] D.O.E. Circular 28/83.
[62] 1976–1977; H.C. 195, p. 11 and Consultative Document Redress Procedures under Codes of Practice (1980) Office of Fair Trading.
[63] *e.g.* Post Office Users National Council, Annual Report, p. 17 (1980–1981).
[64] H.C. Deb., Vol. 21, col. 25, Written Answers, (March 29, 1982). See Electricity Consumers Council Discussion Paper 14, October 1985.

Telecom is concerned it is a condition of its licence[65] to publish a code of practice in respect of disputes and complaints relating to the provision of services in consultation with the Director of Telecommunications who must also be consulted at least once every three years about the operation of the code.

Other guidelines. The Race Relations Commission will keep the Race Relations Code under review[66] and this must apply to any body whether a government Department or outside body who has power to revise a code.

Increasingly, statutory and non-statutory guidelines are subject to judicial control over their legality and interpretation but in addition they fall within a growing number of watchdog bodies who monitor their operation in individual cases and in general.

---

[65] Condition 27.
[66] (1982–1983) H.C. 319, Government Observations on 5th Report of Employment Committee (1981–1982).

Chapter 4

RATIONALE OF QUASI-LEGISLATION

I. The Voluntary Approach in Relation to Private Individuals

Statutory codes

The main though by no means the only justification for quasi-legislation is the "voluntary approach" *i.e.* the reliance on co-operation and consent in preference to the force of law, though, as we saw, the line between law and quasi-legislation is not clear-cut. The Highway Code is the first illustration of this approach. Its genesis was a recommendation by the Royal Commission on Transport in 1929[1] for a Code of Customs which was first brought to their notice by Sir A. Stanley, the Chairman of the R.A.C., who appeared on behalf of a conference of motor organisations and was elaborated by other witnesses. They thought that in the course of time these customs, though in some cases not possessing the force of law, would become universally respected and obeyed and would do more to ensure safety than any legislation.[2] This was said against a background of antagonism between drivers and sections of the public. Earl Russell, the Government spokesman in the House of Lords, reiterated this view when he said, "If the A.A. and R.A.C. joined forces and represented one motoring body obviously any code issued by them would have very considerable moral weight and would, no doubt, be accepted because it would be supported by the opinion of the public which had to be controlled by it."[3] He was in favour of it having only moral force. He was stating the classic argument for self-regulation being preferable to law. To this he added a further point often reiterated in other contexts that a legal code could not contain suggestions and advice. This argument concerns legal terminology which is bound up with the issue of legal force. These arguments must be seen in the context of the social background of the time where "most of the moneyed and intelligent classes are either motorists or well

[1] Cmnd. 3365.
[2] para. 74.
[3] H.L. Deb., Vol. 75, col. 1518–1519 (December 18, 1929).

disposed towards motoring."[4]

The provision in the Agriculture (Miscellaneous Provisions) Act 1968 for codes for the welfare of livestock was closely modelled on the Road Traffic Act. Its genesis is revealing. The Brambell Committee[5] which preceded the Act recommended mandatory standards for the safeguarding of the welfare of animals to be contained in an Act and regulations made under it enforceable in the courts supplemented by non-statutory advice. The Government accepted the need for legislation and for mandatory standards in certain areas and for the rest it preferred the more flexible approach of codes of practice which would not be directly enforceable. The justification for the rejection of the Report's recommendation was the lack of scientific knowledge which made objective judgments impossible and the need for flexibility to enable modifications to be made.[6] The Brambell Committee had met the flexibility point by recommending that detailed standards be contained in statutory instruments but these would have had mandatory force. The Government's arguments must be set against the background of hostility by farmers to the Report,[7] whereas the codes were criticised by animal welfare organisations.[8] It is true that the codes allow room for new developments to be instituted by the producer and that they provide a testing ground for recommendations which in the light of further knowledge and experience may prove to be suitable subjects for regulations.[9] But the main reason for preferring codes to regulations was given by a subsequent Government in evidence to the Agriculture Committee which stated,

> "they regard persuasion as greatly preferable to compulsion. Their favoured weapon is the non-mandatory Code of Recommendations; they prefer to keep mandatory regulation to a minimum, confining it to matters where 'there is established experience or sound scientific evidence to show that a particular item or procedure causes an animal unnecessary pain or unnecessary distress.' Even where there is legislation, they prefer to deal with breaches as far

[4] Quoted by J.R. Spencer, *Motor cars and the Rule in Rylands* v. *Fletcher: A Chapter of Accidents in the History of Law and Motoring.* [1983] C.L.J. 65, 79.
[5] Cmnd. 2836 (1965), chapter 11.
[6] H.C. Deb., Vol. 733, col. 200 *et seq.*, Written Answers (August 5, 1966).
[7] *e.g.* see H.C. Deb., Vol. 830, col. 1124 (February 8, 1972).
[8] H.C. Deb., Vol. 788, col. 829 (October 20, 1969).
[9] 1980–1981; HC 406, Evidence, p. 2, para. 7.

as possible by caution and advice and to prosecute only wilful or persistent offenders."[10]

The Committee thought that the Department put the onus of proof before having recourse to regulation too high and recommended further candidates for regulation. The Farm Animal Welfare Council is considering all welfare codes to see whether any of the recommendations should be made mandatory by being incorporated into regulations. This would replace the voluntary approach with law.[11]

A similar philosophy was adopted by the Robens Report on Safety and Health at Work.[12] Their central aim was self-regulation by employers and employees and in pursuance of this goal they recommended that statutory regulation should only be used as a last resort when voluntary codes or standards were not sufficient.[13] They were also in favour of non-statutory codes on the practical grounds that they can be prepared more quickly, they need not be couched in such precise language, they are less likely to inhibit new developments and they can be revised more easily. They, therefore, recommended that codes should be prepared or approved by the National Authority for Safety and Health at Work and these should be taken into account in enforcement proceedings and be admissible in evidence. They also recommended that regulations should in some cases explicitly refer to voluntary codes and standards thus incorporating them by reference and giving them legislative force. The Health and Safety at Work Act 1974, as we have seen, implemented these recommendations but the Health and Safety Commission has not exercised its power to approve and issue codes of practice in the way envisaged by the Robens Report. The Commission has not used codes in preference to regulations. Instead, as we have seen, "their policy has been to deal with particular areas of hazard, in a considered order of priority, in packages of regulations, codes, guidance notes and enforcement arrangements, all applied to the objective of controlling the specific hazard."[14] Only a handful of codes of practice have been approved by the Commission and they amplify and provide practical guidance on how to comply with the relevant regulations. The Employment Committee in their report on the

---

[10] *Ibid.* para. 36.
[11] H.C. Deb., Vol. 60, col. 627 (May 18, 1984).
[12] Cmnd. 5034 (1971).
[13] *Ibid.* para. 142 *et seq.*
[14] 1981–1982; H.C. 400, para. 10.

Working of the Health and Safety Commission and Executive were concerned at the slow progress that had been made but were finally convinced that the time spent on consultations to obtain consensus for the proposals was not unreasonable.[15] It is clear, therefore, that the hope of the Robens Committee that codes of practice would be a preferable and speedier mechanism than regulations for implementing safety standards has not been fulfilled. Guidance Notes, which have no statutory status, have been found quicker and more appropriate in some cases to back up the general duties in the Act or general objectives set out in regulations. The control limits for asbestos dust were to be found there but are now to be contained in regulations.[16] This represents the exact reverse of the process envisaged by the Robens Committee, though it could also be seen as an illustration of the use of statutory regulations as a last resort after non-statutory provisions had been found wanting. It is clear, however, that the voluntary approach has been used by the Commission as a supplement to statutory regulation rather than as a substitute. This has been acknowledged by the Commission who see the usefulness of codes for covering detailed points in everyday language and for allowing more flexibility in compliance.[17]

The voluntary approach is central to the philosophy of the Wildlife and Countryside Act 1981. The Government spokesman in the House of Lords when introducing the code of guidance clause and rejecting any legal controls over sites of special scientific interest justified it in these words, "In an endeavour to close a bolthole against a few misguided people we may well antagonise the whole of the farming community, upon whom we rely for co-operation in carrying out the wishes of Parliament."[18] In this context the voluntary approach involves a complex package of controls, compensation provisions as well as a voluntary code of guidance to hold the balance between conservation and farming.

The starting point of the voluntary approach lies in the exemption of agriculture from planning control. Agricultural use is not development and change from one type of farming to another is, therefore, not subject to control. Furthermore, the General Development Order 1977 exempts building and engineering operations on agricultural land within certain limits from the need to obtain planning permission. These rights can

---

[15] *Ibid.*
[16] *Supra*, p. 10.
[17] 1981–1982; H.C. 27, App. 11.
[18] H.L. Deb., Vol. 418, col. 396 (March 2, 1981).

be removed by a direction under Article 4 of the Order by the local planning authority with the consent of the Secretary of State. This power has been used in the interests of conservation.[19] But apart from such exceptional cases the virtual exemption of farming activities from planning control epitomises the voluntary approach, because in the last resort (apart from compulsory purchase powers) there is no power to stop as distinct from delay, a farming operation however detrimental to conservation. The National Farmers' Union has argued that there is a fundamental difference between farming and industrial development because the former involves a positive input so as to achieve conservation which cannot be attained by negative controls.[20] On the other hand the Friends of the Earth would like to see development control over certain major agricultural operations,[21] though they recognised that the obstacles to such a change were political as a Conservative government could not introduce such controls. The Government proposes to amend the exemption for agricultural buildings and works in the new General Development Order[22] but the Environment Committee, as well as the Government, rejected the Friends of the Earth's approach as basically in conflict with the voluntary approach.[23]

The provisions of the Wildlife and Countryside Act 1981 stop short of preventing a farmer using his land to the detriment of conservation. Where the Nature Conservancy Council (N.C.C.) has notified him that the area is a site of special scientific interest (S.S.S.I.) he is criminally liable if he carries out a potentially damaging operation within four months of his giving notice of a proposal to do so.[24] This allows time for the N.C.C. to negotiate a management agreement,[25] or, where agreement cannot be reached within this time-scale and it is necessary to protect the site from damage, ask the Secretary of State to make a nature conservation order.[26] This prohibits the farmer from carrying out a potentially damaging operation for up to 12 months within

---

[19] *e.g.* in the case of the Limpenhoe Marshes in the Broads, see H.C. Deb., Vol. 63, col. 147 (July 3, 1984).

[20] 1984–1985; H.C. 6, Q.212—Evidence to Environment Committee.

[21] *Ibid.* Evidence, p. 40, para. 28 *et seq.*

[22] Cmnd. 9522, para. 2.9—Reponse to the Environment Committee Report on the Wildlife and Countryside Act 1981.

[23] 1984–1985; H.C. 6, para. 17.

[24] s.28, as amended.

[25] Imposing restrictions and providing for compensation.

[26] s.29—only 14 such orders had been made by January, 1985; Cmnd. 9522, para. 2.5.

which the N.C.C. may negotiate a management agreement, buy the land by agreement or as a last resort use its compulsory purchase powers—the only compulsory power it has to stop environmentally damaging operations.[27]

One other power which exists in the case of S.S.S.I.'s notified under section 28 or land subject to a nature conservation order is that the N.C.C. may object to a farm capital grant and the Minister of Agriculture must consider such an objection and consult the Secretary of State for the Environment.[28] Refusal of the grant[29] obliges the N.C.C. to offer the farmer a management agreement but he is free to carry out the development without the grant unless it falls within the time limits of a stop order. A similar power to object to such grants exists in the case of land in National Parks or other land specified by Ministers[30] (The Broads have been so specified[31]). In these cases there is not even the temporary stop power which exists in S.S.S.I.'s to spur the farmer into a management agreement.[32]

The main incentive for a farmer to enter a management agreement with the N.C.C. or National Park authority is the compensation obtainable under the financial guidelines for foregoing the potentially damaging operation.[33] This includes the subsidy or grant which the farmer will lose by not carrying out the development. Annual payments are based on profits foregone and will, therefore, go up or down in line with the subsidies which are determined by the Common Agricultural Policy and may be much higher than the value of increased food production.[34] This is the issue on which most criticism has centred, because, in the words of the Friends of the Earth there is "the ridiculous anomaly where M.A.F.F. pay a farmer to do one thing and the Department of Environment pay him to do the opposite."[35] But this anomaly is, as the Environment Committee recognised, "an inevitable and important consequence of the

---

[27] These powers have only been used twice and in neither case in anger; *ibid.* Q.40.
[28] s.32.
[29] There had been only one formal objection by 1984, 1984–1985; H.C. 6, p. 127.
[30] s.41(3)—four cases have been referred to Ministers up to 1984 (one was approved and two refused)—1984–1985; H.C. 6, Evidence, p. 127.
[31] *Ibid.*
[32] *Ibid.* Evidence, p. 105, para. 52 for cases where farmers have gone ahead without a grant.
[33] H.M.S.O. 1983.
[34] 1984–1985; H.C. 6, Evidence, p. 4, para. 18.
[35] *Ibid.* Evidence, p. 41, para. 33.

voluntary approach,"[36] because as Mr. Waldegrave, the Environment Minister, put it, "It would be rather unfair to put the particular farmer who happens to be in a conservation area at a disadvantage just because of that reason, as opposed to the farmer next door who might be getting the grant."[37] As a consequence the conservation budget must bear the cost of agricultural policy in these areas and the cost may be too high for the public body concerned.[38] The only hope lies in falling E.C. subsidies[39] and ultimately in a changed agricultural policy.[40]

The voluntary approach under the Wildlife and Countryside Act is thus an amalgam of temporary stop orders (the stick), voluntary guidance and compensation (the carrot) and of these the last is by far the most important. The cost of the voluntary approach is undoubtedly high.[41] Whether the costs are increased by the sharp practices of some farmers and whether the selfishness of the few is wrecking the Act and discrediting the voluntary approach will be examined later.

The voluntary approach can be seen in a very different context in the code of practice under the Industrial Relations Act 1971. The Act imposed the duty on the Secretary of State to prepare a code containing guidance for the purpose of promoting good industrial relations. Mr. Carr, the then Secretary of State, saw the code within the boundaries of law, playing a positive constructive role in giving guidance to management and unions as to the best practices to follow.[42] Its aim was to enable unions and management to settle their differences by agreement. It would be impossible to embody such practices in the precise terminology of legislation which also would not be flexible enough to allow for frequent revision and supplementation. Opposition to the code by the unions was the result of its association with the Act to which the unions were violently opposed. The T.U.C. drew up its own code, *Good Industrial Relations*, which had a

---

[36] 1984–1985; H.C. 6, para. 14.

[37] *Ibid.* Q.233.

[38] *Ibid.* Evidence, p. 128 paras. 24 and 25.

[39] *Ibid.* Qs. 181 and 182. For cuts in farm capital grants which are environmentally damaging, see H.C. Deb., Vol. 69, col. 433, Written Answers (December 11, 1984).

[40] See 1984–1985; H.C. 6. Evidence, p. 165 for proposals by the National Farmers Union and p. 267 para. 25 and Qs. 348–349 for proposals by the Ministry of Agriculture, and see now Agriculture Act 1986, ss.17–21.

[41] *e.g.* site safeguard including grant aid and land acquisition is costing the N.C.C. £4·5 million in 1984 but these costs are expected to rise steeply as more sites are notified. *Ibid.* Evidence, p. 128, para. 24.

[42] H.C. Deb., Vol. 809, col. 995 (January 19, 1971).

different emphasis but also similarities. Nevertheless the Labour Government, when they returned to power in 1974, retained the code as a result of a Conservative amendment at the Committee Stage of the Trade Union and Labour Relations Bill.[43]

The Labour Government did, however, make new provisions for codes of practice to be issued by A.C.A.S. for promoting the improvement of industrial relations under the Employment Protection Act 1975, s.6. The first Code on Disciplinary Practice and Procedures superseded the relevant provisions of the 1972 Industrial Relations Code. Two further codes have been issued on Disclosure of Information for Collective Bargaining Purposes and Time-Off for Trade Union Duties. Though these caused controversy, the codes aim to be broadly acceptable as a guide to conduct by both sides of industry.

This is one of the crucial differences between the codes under the 1975 Act and the Employment Act 1980 which provided a new power for the Secretary of State to issue codes for the purpose of promoting the improvement of industrial relations. A.C.A.S. refused to comment on the two codes which were issued on Picketing and the Closed Shop because views were divided on them. Apart from outlining the legal provisions of the Act in non-technical terms, the codes give "practical guidance." In a highly controversial area where no agreement about "best practices" is possible, the recommended practices are those which the Government thinks best but which go further than the provisions of the Act. The intention is over a period of time to bring about a change in people's attitude and behaviour, but where these practices are strongly objected to by one side of industry and not wholly acceptable to the other, this is a forlorn hope.[44] Guidance of this nature with the legal backing given in the Act is open to the charge of being back-door legislation especially when such provisions are then embodied in subsequent legislation. They represent a political compromise between those who wanted to go further and those who did not; this then becomes the real *raison d'être* for the codes.

The code of practice under the Race Relations Act 1976 was modelled on the Industrial Relations Code. The provision for a code was inserted in the Act as a result of a back-bench amendment. Its purpose was to supplement the earlier code so as to give a new impetus to developing positive policies for

[43] Standing Committee E, col. 54 (May 16, 1974).
[44] Substantially the same point was made by A.C.A.S., 1981–1982; H.C. 27, App. 12.

establishing equal opportunities in employment.[45] The code is both descriptive, setting out the requirements of the law, and prescriptive, providing a standard against which the actions of employers, employees, trade unions and employment agencies can be judged. The Commission for Racial Equality which has the responsibility for issuing the code, subject to the approval of the Secretary of State, has representatives from both sides of industry who were in complete agreement on the code.[46] However, concern was expressed by the Engineering Employers' Federation to the Employment Committee when they considered the draft code, that it went beyond describing the provisions of the Act. It considered that it should not include general advice on employment practices which were a matter for individual employers.[47] This view was echoed by the Committee when they reiterated their concern (previously expressed in relation to the codes on Picketing and the Closed Shop) about the constitutional undesirability of proliferating codes of practice which have a quasi-judicial effect.[48] The *raison d'être* of the code is to provide practical guidance to eliminate discrimination and promote equal opportunities, the guidance having the maximum degree of acceptance so as to give it the most persuasive impact. The Chairman of the Commission expressed the opinion in evidence to the Employment Committee that, "No Code of Practice whether legally binding or not is worth the paper it is written on unless it has widespread acceptance."[49]

Voluntary codes

The voluntary approach reaches its apotheosis in the purely voluntary code. These have proliferated at an even greater rate than statutory codes. The only examples examined here are those where the Government has used them as a substitute for codes having legal force or conversely where the Government has bowed to pressure (or not as the case may be) and allowed (or refused) voluntary codes to be superseded by legal provisions. Our concern[50] is not self-regulation as such but the rationale of voluntary codes in contrast to legal provisions.

[45] Standing Committee A, col. 737 (June 22, 1976). ·
[46] 1981–1982; H.C. 273, para. 12—Employment Committee Report. The same point was true of the Equal Opportunities Commission's Code of Practice; 1984–1985; H.C. 59.
[47] *Ibid.*, para. 14.
[48] *Ibid.*, para. 18.
[49] *Ibid.*, Q.12.
[50] See Page, [1980] J.B.L. 24, *Self-Regulation and Codes of Practice.*

The Code of Good Practice on the Employment of Disabled People 1985[51] is a purely voluntary code but is set in the context of statutory provisions. The Disabled Persons (Employment) Act 1944 imposed a duty on employers of 20 or more people to employ a quota of registered disabled persons unless they hold an exemption permit because there are insufficient registered disabled people available for the work. This Act has become virtually a dead letter because of the reluctance of disabled people to register, the increase in the number of permits issued and the reluctance of the Manpower Services Commission to enforce the scheme.[52] They, therefore, recommended legislation, modelled on the Health and Safety at Work Act 1974, whereby a general statutory duty "to take reasonable steps to promote equality of employment opportunity for disabled people" would be imposed on employers of 20 or more people and a code of practice would give guidance about the nature of the obligation which would be taken into account in an industrial tribunal or court of law as well as providing guidance on policy and practical matters. Failure to comply with the statutory duty would be an offence but prosecutions would be brought only by the M.S.C., who would only use it as a last resort. This method of enforcement, it was argued, "would be most in line with the thinking that education and persuasion should form the mainstay of future policy for disabled people,"[53] and would avoid the possibility of the employers' goodwill being eroded by less selective litigation. The Employment Committee[54] in their report on the Review wished to be reassured on certain problems before recommending the adoption of the scheme. The Government responded by keeping the existing legislation in being but asked the Manpower Services Commission to draft a code in consultation with interested parties and taking account of the comments received.[55] This, the Secretary of State thought, would enable the usefulness of the code to be tested on a purely voluntary basis without prejudice to its ultimate status. When evidence was taken from the Minister about this code by the Employment Committee, it was put to him by Mr. Janner that unless the code was given the same force as the Race Relations

[51] Chadwick-Healey, 85.332.
[52] M.S.C.—Review of Quota Scheme for Employment of Disabled People—A Report (1981). No prosecutions have been brought since 1975.
[53] *Ibid.* chap. 8.32.
[54] 1981–1982; H.C. 27.
[55] H.C. Deb., Vol. 28, col. 659, Written Answers (July 29, 1982).

and Equal Opportunities Codes it was likely to be nothing more than "governmental wallpaper."[56]

Another area where the Government has opted for voluntary codes in preference to ones having legal force is data protection. The Lindop Committee on Data Protection[57] recommended a scheme for the registration of data users combined with legally enforceable codes of practice drafted by the Data Protection Authority in consultation with users. Some fifty or more codes were envisaged which would apply the general principles in the Act to the wide variety of situations in which personal data are processed automatically. The Government rejected this approach in its White Paper[58] as being too costly and time-consuming but saw some value in voluntary codes drawn up by professional bodies and trade associations. The Government finally gave way to pressure and amended the Bill to impose a duty on the Registrar to encourage trade associations or other bodies representing users to prepare and disseminate to their members codes of practice for guidance in complying with the data protection principles.[59] But the Government firmly rejected any attempt to impose a duty on the Registrar to draw up codes of practice or for them to have any legal standing or evidential value.[60] To adapt Mr. Janner's elegant phrase the codes are likely to be nothing more than "representative wallpaper."[61]

A stronger version of this type of code is provided for in the licence granted to British Telecom. One of the conditions of the licence[62] imposes the duty on B.T. to ensure that its employees engaged in the Systems Business observe a code of practice approved by the Director of Telecommunications regulating the disclosure of information about a customer.

The provision in the Data Protection Act 1984 relating to codes of practice was modelled on the Fair Trading Act 1973, s.124(3) which imposes a duty on the Director of Fair Trading to encourage trade associations to prepare and disseminate to their members codes of practice for guidance in safeguarding and promoting the interests of consumers. Like the amendment in the Data Protection Act, this section was a watered-down version of an amendment rejected during the passage of the

---

[56] 1984–1985; H.C. 32i, Q.36.
[57] Cmnd. 7341 (1978).
[58] Cmnd. 8539 (1982), para. 8.
[59] Data Protection Act 1984, s.36(4).
[60] H.C. Deb., Vol. 61, col. 214 *et seq.* (June 5, 1984).
[61] For a similar view see Austin, [1984] P.L. 618, 631.
[62] Condition 38, H.M.S.O. (1984).

Bill,[63] which would have imposed a duty on the Director to produce the codes. These codes of which 21 had been produced by 1984, have no legal standing.[64] They have been described by the Director as bringing benefits to the consumer which it would be difficult to secure by legislation and to be a compromise between what the consumer considers desirable and the industry considers practicable.[65] Though, as we have seen, the Director is concerned with the monitoring of these codes, their enforcement is dependent on the trade associations exercising their disciplinary powers. They are, therefore, a classic illustration of self-regulation, albeit under statutory provisions.[66]

Voluntary codes can also be used as a staging post to statutory regulation which can be held in reserve as a threat *in terrorem* to ensure their observance. This was the approach used by the Government to persuade the T.U.C. to issue guidelines governing the payment of the political levy by trade unionists. The retention of contracting out of the levy (rather than contracting in which applied between 1927 and 1946) is contingent on the guidelines, which explain the rights of members of trade unions to contract out, being observed by the unions.[67] The Trade Union Act 1984 has meanwhile no provisions on this matter.

This is also the way in which the Government hopes to enforce speed limits for coaches on dual carriageways and motorways. When regulations increasing the speed limit on dual carriageways were introduced it was announced that a voluntary code of conduct had been agreed with the Bus and Coach Council (the operators' national body) which would include the use of tachographs and their monitoring by management to make sure that drivers do not exceed the speed limit.[68] The Secretary of State threatened to take further action if the voluntary code did not work.

The pressure for legislation need not come from the Government. There has been a recurring pattern of a public outcry over some social evil which is met in the first place by the drawing up

---

[63] Standing Committee B, col. 1205 (April 10, 1973).

[64] It will, however, be one of the functions of the Director-General to have regard to the provisions of voluntary codes in considering whether or not a practice should properly be proscribed or proposed for proscription as unfair; *ibid.* col. 1208.   [65] 1976–1977; H.C. 195, p. 11.

[66] The Director-General is looking into the question of enforcement, H.L. Deb., Vol. 452, col. 769 (June 7, 1984), and see Page [1980] J.B.L. 24.

[67] H.C. Deb., Vol 54, col. 686 (February 21, 1984). *Employment News* (March 1984).

[68] H.C. Deb., Vol. 55, cols. 942–943 (March 7, 1984), and see now H.C. Deb., Vol. 86, col. 795 (November 15, 1985) and H.C. Deb., Vol. 97, col. 281, Written Answers (May 9, 1986).

of a code of practice by bodies representing those being pilloried, followed in some cases by legislation. Thus embryo research is being carried out under a code of practice drawn up by the Medical Research Council but a statutory licensing authority has been recommended by the Warnock Committee.[69] Again the Video Recordings Act 1984, a private member's Bill, provides a statutory scheme for the classification of video recordings with heavy fines for breach which supersedes the voluntary code drawn up by the trade associations which was regarded as insufficient by the sponsor of the Bill. Similarly in the case of glue-sniffing the Government at first refused to support legislation and preferred to rely on voluntary guidelines to shops selling solvents which could be bought for sniffing.[70] Over a year later it changed its mind and declared its support for legislation to ban the sale of solvents which could be inhaled for intoxication to young people.[71] The Intoxicating Substances (Supply) Act 1985 gives effect to such a ban. In the case of straw burning by farmers, which gave rise to much controversy, the National Farmers' Union drew up guidelines which were progressively tightened. Model bye-laws imposing penalties drawn up by the Home Office were also strengthened and widely adopted by rural local authorities.[72] Several Bills to ban straw burning have been introduced in the House of Lords and one completed all its stages there,[73] only to be rejected by the Government when they reached the House of Commons. The latest Bill was withdrawn by its sponsor in the House of Lords in the hope that it would be passed in the Commons, as it stood no chance of becoming law otherwise.[74]

An attempt to give the Secretary of State powers to control the advertising of cigarettes was similarly unsuccessful when a private member's Bill was talked out.[75] Advertising of cigarettes except on television and radio is governed by a voluntary agreement between the D.H.S.S., the manufacturers and importers of cigarettes and the Advertising Standards Authority. The 1982 agreement[76] included a price tag of £11 million contributed

---

[69] Cmnd. 9314. [70] *The Guardian*, December 16, 1983.
[71] H.C. Deb., Vol. 59, col. 210, Written Answers (May 3, 1984).
[72] H.C. Deb., Vol. 50, col. 812 *et seq.* (December 12, 1983), and H.C. Deb., Vol. 65, col. 796 (October 25, 1984).
[73] H.L. Deb., Vol. 451, col. 875 (May 8, 1984).
[74] H.L. Deb., Vol. 460, col. 1312 (March 6, 1985).
[75] H.C. Deb., Vol. 27, col. 608 (July 9, 1982).
[76] H.C. Deb., Vol. 29, col. 437, Written Answers (October 27, 1982). New, tougher agreement now reached, see H.C. Deb. Vol. 94, col. 372, Written Answers (March 24, 1986).

by the industry to health research but specifically excluded
research into the use and effects of tobacco. The weakness of the
Government's bargaining position was also evident from a
failure to get the industry to agree to a tougher health warning
than "Smoking is dangerous to health."[76a] It did, however,
achieve a ban on cigarette advertising from video cassettes.

Advertising, except on television[77] and radio, is one of the
most important areas where conduct is governed by self-
regulatory, voluntary codes. The code was first published in
1962. It was drawn up by the Code of Advertising Practice
Committee, consisting of nominees of the trade and professional
associations in consultation with the Advertising Standards
Authority, which has an independent chairman and two-thirds
of whose members are independent of any advertising interest.
There is a separate code of practice administered by the
Association of the British Pharmaceutical Industry for promotion of medicines to the medical profession. Many breaches of
this code have come to light and the Minister has been urged to
use his legal powers to prosecute under the Regulations made
under the Medicines Act 1968.[78] The working of the code came
under fire after the withdrawal of the arthritis drug *Opren*. This
also led to the drawing up of a new code of practice by the
A.B.P.I. in consultation with the Royal College of General
Practitioners and the B.M.A. to regulate clinical trials of new
drugs after they have been marketed by setting up ethical
committees to monitor the way in which drug firms pay G.P.s to
carry out trials and includes guidelines on reporting adverse
reactions and patient selection and consent.[79] The Opposition
spokesman on health called for an independent monitoring body
instead of a voluntary code.[80] There is no national code of
conduct governing clinical trials on healthy volunteers which
may be monitored by hospital ethical committees. The industry
has a voluntary code of practice on compensation. There was
much criticism of this system as the result of the death of Phillip
Jones, a medical student who was taking part in a clinical trial.
The Medicines Commission asked the Royal College of Physi-
cians to recommend safeguards. Inevitably there has been

[76a] The new agreement provides for stronger warnings.
[77] Where statutory backing was given to the voluntary arrangement which
  operated when the service opened in 1955, see Independent Broadcasting Act
  1973, s.9, and see *supra* p. 17.
[78] H.C. Deb., Vol. 57, col. 277, Written Answers (March 29, 1984).
[79] H.C. Deb., Vol. 35, col. 1098 *et seq.* (January 27, 1983).
[80] *The Guardian*, January 29, 1985.

pressure for legislation.[81]

Whether such pressure is successful is very much a matter of politics. It can be no coincidence that legislation to restrict straw burning, advertising and the drugs industry has been opposed by a Conservative Government and that it was a Labour Government which allowed the T.U.C. Codes on picketing and emergency cover to act as a substitute for legislation and which had to resort to indirect means to enforce its White Paper on Incomes Policy. It would be too cynical, however, to regard all voluntary codes as the price a Government has to pay for political support from a vested interest. Self-regulation can be a more effective control mechanism than statutory controls,[82] and even purely voluntary codes can be more than waste paper or governmental wallpaper where there is a reservoir of goodwill, acceptance and a sense of social responsibility and as a corollary trust. Because these criteria are more likely to be present in the case of public authorities quasi-legislation has played such a dominant role in regulating their conduct.

---

[81] H.C. Deb., Vol. 79, col. 112, Written Answers (May 14, 1985).

[82] Page, *op. cit.* p. 27. Professor Gower in his Review of Investor Protection Cmnd. 9125 (1984) opted for self-regulation by the City within a statutory framework of regulation by a governmental agency. He did not recommend regulation through a Securities Commission partly because it would not be practical politics, not only due to party politics but because of opposition from the City. (Discussion Document para. 7.08, H.M.S.O. (1982)). For the latest proposals, see Part II—Review of Investor Protection, H.M.S.O. (1985) and the Financial Services Bill 1986.

Chapter 5

RATIONALE OF QUASI-LEGISLATION

II. The Voluntary Approach in Relation to Public Authorities

Statutory codes

Where quasi-laws (*i.e.* rules which are not legally binding) are
addressed to public authorities the so-called "voluntary approach" as the justification for their use has a different
connotation. For it means that the public body is not legally
bound to the same extent as if the rules were statutory. This is, as
we have seen,[1] a matter of degree for there is no absolute
criterion for legal force and quasi-law can have varying degrees
of bindingness. But this still leaves an important difference
between embodying rules in a statute and, for example, in a code
of practice. This issue was discussed at length during the debates
on both the Police and Criminal Evidence Bills. Time and time
again the Opposition probed the rationale for putting provisions
in the codes of practice rather than the Bill. The Minister of
State, whilst admitting that there was an element of subjectivity
drew this distinction,

> "It has to be a workmanlike attempt at best to say what is
> part of the fundamental rights and duties—the frame-
> work—that the Bill seeks to lay down as a substitute for the
> rather jumbled mishmash that led to the setting up of the
> Royal Commission in the first place, and what actually goes
> to putting flesh on the skeleton but lays down mechanisms
> and procedures that come off the page and provide a
> workable routine for a police officer to follow."[2]

This distinction between substance and procedure or fundamental issues and detail does not, however, fully explain the
difference between what is in the Bill and the codes. The
distinction between matters of substance and procedure or
between fundamental issues and details could just as logically
lead to a dividing line between the Bill and statutory instruments

[1] Chapter 2.
[2] Standing Committee E, col. 1528 (March 1, 1984).

made under the Bill.[3] The difference lies in enforceability and the language which is appropriate for enforcement.[4]

The former distinction is highlighted by the appeal made by Gerald Kaufman, the Opposition spokesman, at one point in the debates when he said, "I will make a deal with the Minister immediately. If he is willing to take this out of the code and put it into the Bill, we shall have a much briefer debate on clause 37."[5] Failure to observe the codes does not render a person liable to civil or criminal proceedings but the codes are admissible in evidence and shall be taken into account where the court considers them relevant in civil or criminal proceedings.[6] The most important issue in criminal proceedings to which they will be relevant will be whether breach of the codes will lead to the exclusion of evidence so obtained. This is governed by section 78 of the Act which gives the court discretion to exclude evidence if "having regard to all the circumstances, including the circumstances in which the evidence was obtained, the admission of the evidence would have such an adverse effect on the fairness of the proceedings that the court ought not to admit it." A similar common law discretion applied to evidence obtained in breach of the Judges' Rules which were the precursors of the codes. It was used very sparingly.[7] Failure to observe them also renders a police officer liable to disciplinary proceedings but breach does not *per se* constitute a disciplinary offence.[8] An Opposition amendment to this effect was strenuously resisted by the Government so as to allow an element of discretion and not make every technical breach a disciplinary offence.[9] But this was later contradicted when the Minister stated that there is already a specific disciplinary offence which applies to such breaches, *i.e.* neglect of duty. The discretion is embodied in the words "shall be liable to disciplinary proceedings" *i.e.* "potentially, every duty that is breached carries with it the possibility of a sanction but whether it is applied is a matter for the chief constable and

---

[3] Statutory instruments were recommended by the Royal Commission on Criminal Procedure, Cmnd. 8092 (1981), para. 4.116.

[4] *cf.* Zander, *Police and Criminal Evidence Act* (1984), p. 94.

[5] Standing Committee E, col. 1188 (February 16, 1984). This is a different point from that discussed, *supra* in Chap. 2, n. 12 where the question in issue was whether the Codes as such should be embodied in the Bill.

[6] subs.67(10) and (11).

[7] *Kuruma* v. *The Queen* [1955] A.C. 197, *Jeffrey* v. *Black* [1977] 3 W.L.R. 895, *R.* v. *Lemsatef* [1977] 1 W.L.R. 812, *R.* v. *Sang* [1979] 3 W.L.R. 263.

[8] s.67(8).

[9] Standing Committee E, col. 1544, (March 1, 1984).

his advisers."[10] Therefore, creating a specific disciplinary offence for breach of the codes would not seem to add anything to their enforceability.

Closely related to the question of enforceability is the language in which the codes are couched. There were frequent references by the Government spokesmen during the debates to the freer language of the codes,[11] the more relaxed way in which matters could be dealt within the codes[12] and that the codes were more flexible than the law.[13] All this is tantamount to saying that the Government is prepared to put further safeguards for the individual in the codes because they are written in looser language and do not have the same force as statutory provisions. The codes are, in fact, a mixture, some parts merely repeat the statutory provisions, other parts *e.g.* those on questioning and identification, have no counterpart in the Act, but embody in amended form previous non-statutory provisions. The remaining parts supplement the provisions of the Act providing safeguards for the individual in addition to those in the Act. For this reason the Opposition made strenuous efforts to have provisions transposed into the Bill and this led Mr. Mikardo to make the not wholly accurate gibe on the first occasion the Bill went through Committee, that the powers of the police were in the Bill while the rights of the person were in the codes.[14] Even if this is not accepted as the rationale for dividing the provisions between the codes and the Act, the voluntary approach when applied to police powers deprives the individual of rights rather than absolving him from duties.[15]

Further, the arguments in favour of flexibility and informality are capable of infinite regression. Thus the Government originally rejected a code relating to search of premises and seizure of property on very similar grounds to those on which it rejected proposals to put provisions in the Act rather than the codes. They argued that the codes have prescriptive force and that the way in which a search is conducted depended on an infinite number of variables which would have to be decided by the

---

[10] *Ibid.* col. 1548.
[11] *Ibid.* col. 1527.
[12] *Ibid.* col. 1560.
[13] *Ibid.* col. 899.
[14] Standing Committee J, col. 1013 (March 1, 1983).
[15] The same considerations apply to the code of practice to be issued in connection with the tape recording of interviews with suspects under s.60 of the Act which will have the same degree of enforceability as the codes under s.66.

officer on the spot.[16] The Government later changed its mind
and drafted a code for searching premises and seizure of
property when the second Bill was presented after the General
Election. They also eventually gave in to pressure to draft a code
relating to the powers to stop and search people and vehicles.[17]

Another recent example where legal provisions have been
supplemented by a code of practice, but one which has no
statutory force, is contained in the Mental Health (Amendment)
Act 1982. Following the recommendation in the White Paper,[18]
the Act[19] imposes a duty on the Secretary of State[20] to draw up a
code in relation to the medical treatment of mental patients. In
this he must specify forms of medical treatment in addition to
those specified in regulations which give rise to special concern
and should, therefore, be given with the consent of the patient
and subject to special safeguards. The justification for not listing
these treatments in the regulations was the usual one of the
difficulty of giving precise legal definition to all such treatments
and the ability to revise the code to take account of new and
changing forms of treatment. The Confederation of Health
Service Employees (C.O.H.S.E.) not surprisingly pressed for all
treatments to be contained in the regulations.[21] The Mental
Health Act Commission has not recommended so far any
additional forms of treatment to be contained in the code.[22] In
response to an amendment introduced in the House of Lords[23]
the Government widened the scope of the code of practice under
section 53 to include guidance in relation to the admission of
patients to mental hospitals. This guidance will supplement the
legal provisions of the Act but have no legal force.

In the Health and Social Services and Social Security

---

[16] Standing Committee J, col. 1065, March 3, 1983 *et seq.* In this context it is
interesting to note that the codes now include "Notes for Guidance" which are
not provisions of the code but are guidance to police officers and others about
its application and interpretation, see Code of Practice for Detention *etc.*
para. 1.3. Breach of these provisions does not presumably rank as breach of the
code under s.67, see also Zander, *op. cit.*, p. 95–96. Further guidance will be
issued to all police officers by Home Office circular as to how the codes should
operate, H.C. Deb., Vol. 88, col. 488 (December 5, 1985).

[17] s.66(*a*), (*c*) and (*d*).   [18] Cmnd. 8405, para. 38.

[19] s.53; see now Mental Health Act 1983, s.118.

[20] The Code will be drawn up by the Mental Health Act Commission. A draft
code has been published; H.M.S.O. 1986.

[21] Special Standing Committee, col. 102, April 27, 1982.

[22] 1984–1985; H.C. 586—1st Biennial Report. No agreement about such treatments could be reached even among the Commissioners.

[23] H.L. Deb., Vol. 426, col. 849 (January 25, 1982) and H.L. Deb., Vol. 427,
col. 1072 (February 25, 1982).

Adjudications Act 1983, s.6 and Schedule 1 there is another statutory provision for a code of practice to supplement the legal right of a parent to appeal against a local authority's refusal to allow access to a child in the authority's care. The code of practice drawn up by the Secretary of State[24] sets out good social work practice in relation to access to all children in care including those in voluntary care.[25] Again, it was said that the wide range of problems involved could not be dealt with in detailed primary legislation and not all problems could be solved by narrow legal changes. Though the Act provides for consultation, publication and annulment by either House (like the code under the Mental Health Act), there are no provisions for enforcement, though there is the legal right of appeal against the local authority's refusal of access. The voluntary approach is not used here as an alternative to creating legal rights but the legal right is available as a reserve weapon if the voluntary code has failed to resolve the issue.

The same arguments which the Government used in favour of the statutory code of practice for access to children in care in preference to legislation were used during the passage of the Bill to support non-statutory codes of guidance relating to standards to be observed in private residential care and nursing homes. It was said that it would be impractical to embody detailed provisions in the Bill because of a widely differing range of accommodation and such provisions would also lead to inflexibility[26]. However, unlike the code of practice for access to children, no provisions for the making, publication or consulta-

---

[24] Local Authority Circular L.A.C. (83)19.

[25] Standing Committee B, col. 755 (April 28, 1983).

[26] H.C. Deb., Vol. 37, col. 533 (February 17, 1983). The same arguments were again used by the Government to resist statutory standards for prisons in reply to an amendment at the Committee stage of the Criminal Justice Bill (H.L. Deb., Vol. 431, col. 1001 *et seq.* (June 22, 1982)). But the real reason for resisting statutory standards seems to have been the difficulty of complying with them unless they were set inordinately low. The certified normal accommodation which is set for each prison at present is almost invariably exceeded. The Government did, however, concede the case for a non-statutory code of standards setting a target along the lines of the standard minimum rules for the treatment of prisoners laid down by the United Nations and Council of Europe. Because of the delay by the Government in producing such a code both the prison governors (*The Guardian*, September 30, 1984) and the National Council for the Care and Resettlement of Offenders (*The Guardian*, March 23, 1984) have drawn up their own codes of standards. H.M. Inspector of Prisons has embarked on a review of work being done in other countries with the aim of establishing more objective standards of assessment. (1984–1985; H.C. 589 para. 3.01).

tion in respect of the codes were put into the Bill. Instead, the Government accepted an offer from a charity to draw up a code for residential homes[27] and from the National Association of Health Authorities to do likewise for nursing homes.[28] The aim was to promote more consistency of standards[29] and to lay down standards as to quality of care which do not lend themselves to legal regulation. As we saw, the codes, though non-statutory, do have indirect legal force as standards to which regard will be had by authorities responsible for the registration and inspection of such homes[30] and in the case of residential care homes the code ranks as general guidance issued by the Secretary of State under the Local Authority Social Services Act 1970, s.7 to local authorities for the exercise of their social services functions. The recommendations in the code are discretionary rather than mandatory for local authorities.

By this route the non-statutory code drawn up by a private body is given the same force *vis-à-vis* local authorities as the statutory code of guidance made under section 12 of the Housing (Homeless Persons) Act 1977 to which local authorities must have regard in exercising their functions in relation to the homeless. As was decided in *de Falco* v. *Crawley Borough Council*,[31] such guidance is not binding on the local authority. Guidance had previously been contained in a circular,[32] which was held to be a relevant consideration for the authority to take into account when exercising its discretion to give notice to quit to a council house tenant.[33] This code exemplifies a growing trend to make statutory provision for guidance to be issued by central government to local authorities which has traditionally been contained in non-statutory circulars. Other recent examples include the code of practice on local government audit which was originally non-statutory[34] but which was given a statutory basis by the Local Government Finance Act 1982, s.14,[35] the codes of recommended practice as to publication of information by local authorities under section 2 of the Local Government, Planning and Land Act 1980 and the guidance to which local authorities must have regard in discharging their

[27] *Home Life.*
[28] A Handbook for Health Authorities.
[29] H.C. Deb., Vol. 37, col. 496 (February 17, 1983).
[30] Standing Committee B, col. 387, March 29, 1983; see *supra*, Chap. 2, n. 76.
[31] [1980] 2 W.L.R. 664; *supra*, Chap. 2, n. 64.
[32] D.O.E. 18/74.
[33] *Bristol District Council* v. *Clark* [1975] 1 W.L.R. 1443.
[34] D.O.E. Circular 79/73, Annex II.
[35] It is now prepared by the Audit Commission.

duty to consult industrial and commercial ratepayers under section 13 of the Rates Act 1984. These provisions have not enhanced the status of such guidance over that contained in circulars, as the codes have been given persuasive rather than binding force.[36] Therefore, unlike the provisions to be examined in the next section, they do not override the consensual relationship between central and local government. They can, however, formalise it by providing procedural safeguards such as laying before Parliament and duties to consult and publish. This has been done in several cases.[37] Thus they are examples of the voluntary approach which has until recently been the hall-mark of central-local relations.

This trend towards greater formalisation of guidance through statutory provisions can also be seen in relation to the police.[38] Thus the Transport Act 1982, s.51 provides that the Secretary of State shall issue guidance to chief officers of police in respect of the operation of fixed penalty offences, with the objective so far as possible of working towards uniformity. The Government strongly resisted earlier amendments to the Bill which would have made such advice legally binding.[39] The Government felt that uniformity would have to be achieved gradually rather than instantaneously, that a circular would allow flexibility whereas legally binding advice would act as a strait-jacket and that it was normal practice to issue advice to chief constables in the expectation that it would be followed but not to give it statutory force. These are once more the classic arguments for the voluntary approach. The novelty is that the Government gave way to pressure and included a provision for guidance in the Act. This also happened in the case of the Police and Criminal Evidence Bill with regard to guidance concerning liaison between the police and the community. Following the recom-

---

[36] *de Falco* v. *Crawley Borough Council, supra,* n. 31. See also the guidance under s.7 of the Local Authority Social Services Act 1970. A new recruit will be added under the Local Government Act 1986, s.4 which provides for codes of recommended practice in respect of local authority publicity.

[37] *i.e.* the code of practice for access to children in care, the mental health code and the audit code. The Local Government Bill 1986, s.4 provides for parliamentary approval and consultation. The Local Government, Planning and Land Act 1980, s.3 provides for consultation.

[38] The codes under the Police and Criminal Evidence Act 1984 raise more fundamental issues, see *supra,* p. 66.

[39] Standing Committee F, col. 1056 (April 22, 1982) and H.C. Deb., Vol. 24, col. 829 (May 25, 1982). Home Office circulars have been issued, H.L.Deb., Vol. 470, col. 541 (January 28, 1986).

mendations of the Scarman Report on the Brixton Disorders such guidance had been contained in a non-statutory circular.[40] When the first Police Bill imposed the duty on police authorities to make arrangements for consulting the community, the Home Secretary came under pressure to lay down statutory guidelines. He resisted this on the familiar ground of keeping flexibility but compromised by providing for guidance to be issued by him in the Metropolitan Police area for which he is the police authority. This had hardened into a duty to issue guidance in the second Bill.[41] In the rest of the country the guidance will continue to be non-statutory. All attempts at specifying criteria to be contained in the guidance in the Act were rejected in the interests of flexibility but very residual sanctions were conceded in the form of a power in the Secretary of State to call for a report where he considers the arrangements inadequate and a further power to require a review of the arrangements and another report.[42]

A similar progression from non-statutory to statutory guidance occurred in connection with guidance to the police concerning discipline and complaints against the police. This guidance had been contained in a circular[43] but it was put on a statutory footing during the passage of the first Bill through Parliament. Strenuous efforts were made by Mr. Eldon Griffiths, the spokesman for the Police Federation, to make the guidance binding on the police rather than merely being obliged to have regard to it. This was strongly resisted by the Government, partly on the ground that guidance could be more detailed than binding rules[44] but more importantly for the reason given by the Minister of State when introducing the amendment to the first Bill, "If he [Mr. Griffiths] wants chief police officers and other senior officers throughout the whole country to be subject to specific instructions from the Home Secretary on their operations, he is asking for a national police force."[45] It is concern for

---

[40] See H.C. Deb., Vol. 25, col. 281, Written Answers (June 16, 1982) and Home Office Circular 54/82. For the implementation of this circular which varied greatly, see Birkinshaw, *Grievances, Remedies and the State*, p. 159 *et seq.*

[41] Police and Criminal Evidence Act, s.106. The guidelines are contained in Home Office Circular 1985/2, available from the Home Office library.

[42] s.106 (10) and (11).

[43] 32/80—See *R.* v. *Police Complaints Board ex p. Madden and Rhone* [1983] 1 W.L.R. 447, *supra*, p. 15. Revised Guidance was issued in Cmnd. 9072 (1983).

[44] Standing Committee E, col. 1942–1943 (March 22, 1984).

[45] Standing Committee J, col. 1435 (March 24, 1983). Enforceability of the guidance was strengthened on the Report Stage of the second Police Bill by making failure to have regard to the guidance admissible in evidence on an appeal; see s.105(3) of the Police and Criminal Evidence Act 1984.

the autonomy of local police forces that has made governments so careful not to make guidance issued to encourage uniformity legally binding. The recent examples of putting such guidance on a statutory basis were concessions made in response to pressure from those who wanted more legal force to be given to the guidance. The Government, however, refused to bring lay visiting of police stations within the scope of the Bill, because the scheme was still at the experimental stage.[46] Guidelines for the establishment of such schemes are contained in a Home Office circular.[47] Traditionally guidance to the police has been purely non-statutory and taken the form of Home Office circulars. This is still the normal mechanism for guidelines from the Home Secretary. Recently such guidelines have been given on firearms issues following the shooting of Mr. Stephen Waldorf by police officers in mistake for another man.[48] Guidance has also been issued on the handling of rape complaints.[49]

Recently the issuing of guidelines to the police forces to bring about uniformity has been extended to prosecution policies. The Attorney-General in response to the recommendations of the Royal Commission on Criminal Procedure issued guidelines because there was too much disparity between the 43 police services.[50] He has also issued guidelines for more consistent use of the caution.[51] These guidelines have been published but, unlike the guidance on fixed penalty offences under the Transport Act 1982, they have no statutory basis. In contrast, the guidelines issued to Chief Constables in July 1977 on the use of bugging devices only came to light as a result of the discovery of a bug in a telephone box in North Wales.[52] After being leaked to *The Guardian* they were placed in the library of the House of Commons in February 1982.[53] The publication of the Home Office guidelines on the nature and duties of the Special Branch in December 1984 was regarded by the Home Affairs

---

[46] Standing Committee J, col. 929 (February 24, 1983).
[47] *The Guardian*, September 2, 1985 and H.C. Deb., Vol. 65, col. 222, Written Answers (July 31, 1984).
[48] Circular 1983/47—available from the Home Office library.
[49] Circular 1983/25—available from the Home Office library.
[50] H.L. Deb., Vol. 439, col. 92 (February 14, 1983). They have been placed in the library of both Houses. They recommended that there should be at least a 50 per cent. chance of conviction.
[51] A circular was issued in February 1985.
[52] H.C. Deb., Vol. 17, col. 481, Written Answers (February 12, 1982).
[53] H.C. Deb., Vol. 18, col. 452, Written Answers (February 25, 1982).

Committee as a major offshoot of their inquiry into the Police Special Branch.[54] The Attorney-General's guidelines on jury vetting issued in a Home Office circular to Chief Constables in 1975[55] were not published until 1978. It was then said that they were not included in the Juries Act 1974 because "the guidelines are a means of controlling an administrative practice which is inappropriate for legislation."[56] There are now a number of precedents for including a provision in legislation for the issuing of such guidance to the police, though in none of these examples has the provision enhanced parliamentary control.

Non-statutory guidelines

Non-statutory guidelines have been the normal channel of communication and control by central government over local authorities, nationalised industries and health authorities. They have also been used ever more extensively by all public authorities to structure their own discretion. We will concentrate mainly on those guidelines which have been superseded by legal provisions or where there has been pressure for this to happen and those which supplement or conflict with legal provisions. Thus the rationale of non-statutory guidelines in contrast to legal provisions will be explored.

Local government. A history of local government could be written around the transformation of persuasive guidelines into statutory provisions. Nowhere has this been more marked than in the realm of local government finance where recent legislation represents the high-water mark of the transformation of the relationship between central and local government from one of exhortation, encouragement and advice backed up by monetary incentives and disincentives to one of statutory prescription with legal sanctions.

Until 1980 central government had no control over how much individual local authorities could spend. Before that date the Labour Government sought to restrain the total of local authority expenditure by reduction of the central government grant and by exhortation through circulars to local authorities to remain within the targets set by central government. In 1980 the

---

[54] 1984–1985; H.C. 363, p. xliv, para. 7—Liaison Committee Report.
[55] Home Office Circular 165/1975.
[56] See H.C. Deb., Vol. 959, col. 30, Written Answers (November 27, 1978). The lack of parliamentary authority for a practice which has profound implications for civil liberties is open to severe criticism, see East (1985) M.L.R. 518, 530.

Local Government, Planning and Land Act for the first time gave the government power to determine the expenditure needs of each local authority in the form of the grant related expenditure assessment (G.R.E.A.). This was said to be purely a mechanism for grant distribution not an expenditure ceiling. It was the Local Government Finance Act 1982, s.8 which for the first time enabled the government to issue guidance to local authorities setting targets for local authority expenditure (which may be set by reference to G.R.E.A.) in accordance with which the block grant will be distributed. This guidance, therefore, has legal force in that it determines the amount of grant. It did not, however, prevent expenditure above that level. This only came with the Rates Act 1984 which enabled the Secretary of State to determine an expenditure level for designated authorities[57] by reference to which the maximum rate for that authority is then fixed. In this way the government can effectively control the expenditure of rate-capped authorities and it has the power under that Act to rate-cap all authorities.[58] Central government thus now has legal powers to control the expenditure of certain and potentially all local authorities instead of having to rely on exhortation and the manipulation of grants.

Each side has accused the other of breaking long-standing conventions regulating the relationship between central and local government. The government argued that until recently, "Local government observed the implicit understanding that its aggregate expenditure should not exceed the planning totals determined by central government."[59] Local government claims that the government are effecting a fundamental change when they interfere with the power of local authorities to determine their own expenditure and to raise their own rates. Whoever is right, it is clear that consensus has broken down over local government expenditure and the government has resorted to increasingly draconian legislative powers. Whether overspending is attributed mainly to a few authorities or to many depends very much on which criteria one adopts.[60]

It is not, however, only in the realm of local government finance that this development has been taking place. A classic illustration of the same phenomenon is the metamorphosis of

---

[57] Designation may again be by reference to G.R.E.A.
[58] Rates Act 1984, Part II.
[59] Cmnd. 9008, para. 1.11.
[60] Less than 20 authorities have been rate-capped but in 1983–1984, 20 per cent. of authorities spent above target and a much larger percentage spent above G.R.E.A.

the Labour Government's policy on comprehensive schools from departmental circulars to Act of Parliament. On November 27, 1964[61] the Secretary of State said in a debate on grammar schools, "In the Government's view we ought now to accept that reorganisation of secondary education on comprehensive lines should be national policy." This was endorsed by the House of Commons when a Government amendment to an Opposition motion on a Supply Day was approved.[62] In that debate the Secretary of State said that he would not ask for legislative powers unless they were absolutely necessary.[63] In July 1965 the famous Circular 10/65 was issued in which the Secretary of State requested local education authorities who had not already done so to prepare and submit to him plans for reorganising secondary education on comprehensive lines and setting out different methods for achieving this. This was later backed up by Circular 10/66 warning L.E.A.s that no new projects incompatible with a non-selective system of education would receive his approval.[64] It was not till 1976, when Labour had regained power, that legislation was passed giving the Secretary of State power to require the submission of plans for reorganisation on comprehensive lines in order to bring the few[65] recalcitrant authorities to heel. The Opposition raised the constitutional issue of the balance of power between the Secretary of State and the local education authority.[66] The Secretary of State rebutted the charge by claiming that the issue was one of national policy but he added that he would have preferred to deal with the issue by agreement.[67] However, impasse having been reached, he had introduced the Bill.[68] The analogy with the arguments on the Rates Act 1984 is close. The relevant provisions of the 1976 Act were repealed by the Conservative Government by the Education Act 1979.

In contradistinction Government policy to promote school closures in the light of falling numbers of school children has so far been confined to circulars. The first circular drawing attention to the decline in the school population and asking local

[61] H.C. Deb., Vol. 702, col. 1785.
[62] H.C. Deb., Vol. 705, col. 413 (January 21, 1965).
[63] *Ibid.* col. 444.
[64] These circulars were withdrawn by the Conservative Government by Circular 10/70. There was a further circular in 1974 (4/74) issued by the newly elected Labour Government reiterating its policy on comprehensive education.
[65] Seven authorities declared their opposition in principle.
[66] H.C. Deb., Vol. 901, col. 507 (November 24, 1975).
[67] *Ibid.* col. 521.
[68] H.C. Deb., Vol. 904, col. 1219 (February 4, 1976).

authorities to reassess future trends and how to make the best
use of school premises was issued by the Labour Government in
1977 (5/77). This was followed in 1981 by a more peremptory
circular (2/81) from the Conservative Government asking all
L.E.A.s who had not so far embarked on a comprehensive review
to undertake one as a matter of urgency. It also asked every
L.E.A. to inform the Department about the expected number of
surplus places and their plans for taking places out of use. This
information will be taken into account by the Secretary of State
when considering his plans for educational expenditure. This
hint of a financial sanction is complemented by a financial
incentive to take into account the need to improve schools
receiving pupils from closed schools when determining the levels
of capital expenditure for education.

The sale of council houses provides another illustration where
a policy originally embodied in circulars was finally translated
into law. The Conservative Government first gave a general
consent to the sale of council houses under the Housing Act
1957, s.104 in 1970[69] subject to certain conditions. This was
followed by a further circular in 1972[70] expressing concern that,
"many authorities continue to adopt policies which frustrate
their tenants' desire to own their home" and urged "all local
authorities who are reluctant to sell council houses to those
tenants who wish to buy them to reconsider their policies." The
newly elected Labour Government in 1974 contented itself with
a new circular[71] refuting the view that local authorities should
sell their houses indiscriminately whatever the local housing
situation and expressing the view that in the large cities, where
there were substantial needs for rented dwellings, it was
generally wrong to sell council houses. The Secretary of State
exhorted local authorities in the exercise of their discretion in
this matter, to adopt policies in accordance with those views.
The Conservative Government after the 1979 election embodied the "right to buy" in the Housing Act 1980. Since 1979
the Government has increasingly relied on legislation rather
than persuasion to force local authorities to comply with its

---

[69] Circular 54/70—published by the Department but not H.M.S.O. It removed
the restrictions imposed in 1968 on the sale of council houses in certain areas.
It was supplemented by Circular 30/73 following the Housing (Amendment)
Act 1973.
[70] 56/72.
[71] 70/74.

policies.[72] This is fundamentally changing the relationship between central and local government from one based on consensus to one of law.

In the area of planning, however, legislation plays little part in laying down substantive policies. The Acts lay down the framework for making planning decisions ranging from the structure plan at one end of the spectrum to the individual planning application at the other. The General Development Orders which are statutory instruments contain substantive policies in that they determine which development does not require planning permission. Similarly, the Local Government, Planning and Land Act 1980[73] provides for enterprise zones where planning permission is automatically granted for certain classes of development. But most substantive planning policy is contained in circulars and development control policy notes as well as bulletins of planning appeal decisions. The most famous recent illustration is the circular on Green Belt policy[74] which, as we have seen, proved very controversial and was withdrawn and revised after pressure from within and outside Parliament.

The reason why central government does not need to embody its planning policies in statutory form lies in the planning machinery. Structure plans laying down the strategic policy of the area are subject to ministerial approval whilst local plans which lay down the detailed policy may be called in by the Secretary of State. In the case of a unitary development plan prepared by a local authority in a metropolitan area under the Local Government Act 1985 (Schedule 1) the authority must have regard to strategic guidance from the Secretary of State. By this means the Minister can control the planning policy of the local authority. Applications which the local planning authority considers constitute a material departure from the plan have to be notified to the Minister[75] and may then be called in by him[76] though this power is exercised very sparingly. By this means the possibility of granting permission in conflict with the plan can be forestalled. A refusal of planning permission is subject to appeal to the Minister and will, therefore, be decided in accordance

[72] The latest recruit is the Local Government Act 1986 banning political advertising by local authorities and making the fixing of a rate compulsory by a certain date.

[73] Schedule 32.

[74] D.O.E. Circular 14/84.

[75] D.O.E. Circular 2/81, incorporating the T.C.P. (Development Plans) Direction.

[76] Town and Country Planning Act 1971, s.35.

with his policy, though this is affected by delegation of decisions
to inspectors from whom decisions can, however, be recovered
for decision by the Secretary of State.[77] Within this structure the
Secretary of State does not need to promote his substantive
policies through legislation, though wholesale exemptions from
planning control (*e.g.* general development orders and enterprise
zones) or general restrictions on the grant of planning permission (*e.g.* industrial and office development certificates) must be
embodied in an Act.

Procedural rules relating to planning may be contained in
statutory instruments, *e.g.* the rules of procedure relating to
inquiries made under the Tribunals and Inquiries Act 1971, but
even these were modelled on Circular 9/58 which first implemented the recommendations of the Franks Report relating to
inquiries. But many procedural rules are still only embodied in
circulars and codes of practice, *e.g.* the written representation
procedure,[78] the codes of practice for the examination in public
of structure plans[79] and for local plan inquiries,[80] publicity for
planning applications,[81] the code of practice for informal
hearings of planning appeals[82] and for pre-inquiry stages of
major inquiries.[83] The advantage is flexibility, the ability to be
experimental and to use non-technical language. The disadvantage is that the procedure cannot be imposed on individuals
without their consent so that they remain free to use a formal
statutory procedure where this is available. Conversely, where
the non-statutory procedure is not adhered to, individuals have
no legal remedies, though even procedural provisions in statutes
may not be given mandatory force. It is not surprising that the
Council on Tribunals have pressed for statutory rules, pressure
which the department has tried to resist.[84]

Nationalised industries. The relationship between central government and the nationalised industries has also been mainly
based on the voluntary approach, *i.e.* the exercise of informal
ministerial control rather than the use of statutory powers. The

---

[77] *Ibid.* Sched. 9.
[78] Circulars 32/65 and 38/81.
[79] Section 2 of *Structure plans: The Examination in Public—A Guide to Procedure*
(1984).
[80] Section 2 of *Local Plans: Public Local Inquiries—A Guide to Procedure* (1984).
[81] D.O.E. Circular 71/73.
[82] D.O.E. (July 1981).
[83] D.O.E. (June 1984).
[84] Successfully so far in the case of local plan inquiries—see Council on Tribunal
Report for 1979–1980, chap. 6.32 and Report for 1980–1981, chap. 6.23.

best known illustration is the use of the "lunch-table directive," namely informal negotiation between the sponsoring Minister and the Chairman instead of issuing a legal direction "in the public interest" under statutory provisions. Significantly, however, the Secretary of State had to resort to the statutory power and direct the British Gas Corporation to sell off its share in the Wytch Farm oilfield[85] and to sell off its offshore oil interests[86] because of strong opposition from the Corporation. The Wytch Farm direction was later supplemented by an instruction to negotiate with a certain company because the Corporation had not yet found a buyer. Such an instruction has no legal basis and short of issuing a further direction the Secretary of State had to rely on voluntary compliance. It was argued that the sale would be in breach of the Corporation's statutory duty to obtain the best price for any sale of assets and the Select Committee on Energy took evidence on the point from the Corporation and the Department. The Corporation said it had been advised that its duty was to secure a reasonable price taking all the relevant circumstances into account; the Committee felt it could not carry the matter further and that only the courts could resolve any doubts about the legality of the Government's instruction.[87]

The clash between the statutory provisions regulating the industry and the informal controls exercised by the Secretary of State is illustrated most graphically by financial obligations. In the case of the older corporations the overriding financial duty was to break even. This duty was in practice superseded by successive White Papers[88] issued by both Labour and Conservative governments, substituting financial targets for the statutory duty to break even. This gave rise to the gibe of government by White Paper. It was the legality of the financial target set for the British Airports Authority (B.A.A.) which was challenged in *Air Canada* v. *Secretary of State for Trade*[89] as *ultra vires* because it was alleged by the airlines to have been imposed for macro-economic purposes to reduce the Public Sector Borrowing Requirement by making the profitable nationalised industries subsidise the unprofitable ones rather than to enable the B.A.A. to perform its statutory duties. Unfortunately these allegations were never tested in court as the case was settled after the

[85] H.C. Deb., Vol. 9, col. 916 (July 27, 1981).
[86] H.C. Deb., Vol. 29, col. 972 (October 26, 1982) and H.C. Deb., Vol. 47, col. 239 (October 25, 1983).
[87] 1983–1984; H.C. 358.
[88] Cmnd. 1337 (1961), Cmnd. 4027 (1969), Cmnd. 7131 (1978).
[89] [1983] 2 W.L.R. 494.

airlines had failed to obtain discovery of the Government documents they were seeking.

A similar issue arose in respect of the raising of electricity prices after the Secretary of State had fixed an External Financing Limit (E.F.L.) under which the electricity supply industry (E.S.I.) had to make an additional payment to the Treasury which was higher than that required under its financial target. The E.F.L. sets the annual ceiling for finance from sources external to the industry and supplements the financial targets which are set for three to five years as a rule. In the case of the electricity industry the E.F.L. is negative, *i.e.* the amount fixed has to be paid to the Treasury. The Select Committee on Energy which investigated the price increase came to the conclusion "that the only plausible motivation for the large increase in the E.S.I.'s negative E.F.L. for 1984–85 . . . was the Government's wish, on grounds of macro-economic policy, to raise additional revenue in order to reduce the Public Sector Borrowing Requirement."[90] The London Electricity Consumer Council took Counsel's Opinion about the legality of the Government's action. He stated that the statutory duty was to break even and not to make a profit. To generate surpluses which are not required for the legitimate purpose of reserve funds would involve a breach of statutory duties by the Electricity Boards and should therefore be resisted by them. Counsel was also of the opinion that the Electricity Acts did not allow the industry to be used as an instrument for promoting wider economic objectives outside the scope of its own immediate field.[91] Counsel seems, therefore, to be in agreement with the allegations of the airlines in the *Air Canada* case, though again this opinion has not yet been tested in court.[92] What is illustrated by these examples is that the informal controls may be used by the Government not only instead of its statutory powers as in the case of the lunch-table directive but in conflict with the statutory duties of the industry. Up till now there has been no successful challenge to the legality of these Government actions. Doubt about their validity strengthens the hand of a Board in resisting the Government's actions, though it has no duty to comply with such informal non-statutory controls even if they are legal. Conversely, compliance with the Government's edicts cannot

[90] 1983–1984; H.C 276, para. 49.
[91] *Ibid.* p. 58.
[92] In its reply to the Committee's report the Government stated that it understands that the Board have been advised that it would be lawful for them to increase tariffs, 1983–1984; H.C. 417, p. vii.

legalise them. The use of informal directives in conflict with statutory provisions here has the reverse effect from tax concessions. They fall foul of the Bill of Rights not as the exercise of a dispensing power but because, as Counsel's Opinion pointed out in the case of the raising of electricity prices, they amounted to a form of taxation on consumers which had not been authorised by legislation. But quite apart from the Bill of Rights such non-statutory directives, if in contravention of statutory duties, would be *ultra vires*. These possibly illegal controls, however, illustrate the pathology of informal control rather than the norm. A consultation paper issued by the Treasury[93] proposing a common statutory framework for all the nationalised industries including giving statutory backing to financial targets has been unanimously condemned by all the nationalised industries as increasing the power of the Executive over the nationalised industries and restricting their ability to act in a businesslike manner.[94] The Government already has statutory power to give directions by order to Water Authorities fixing a rate of return.[95] On the most recent occasion such an order was made, it was heavily criticised on both sides of the House for the same reason as the non-statutory electricity E.F.L., namely as a form of taxation.[96] Though there is no immediate intention to enact the proposals in the consultation paper,[97] their enactment would greatly accelerate the trend towards regulating the relationship between the government and the nationalised industries by law rather than by consensus in the same way as is happening in the case of local authorities.

National Health Service. The relationship between the Secretary of State and the health authorities is also based primarily on the voluntary approach. The Minister does have power to make regulations by statutory instrument particularly in respect of charges and it was this power which was used to impose charges for overseas visitors.[98] These regulations were accompanied by a manual of guidance and explanation which was annexed to a draft circular to health authorities but which was not referred to in the explanatory note to the statutory instrument, which was

---

[93] December 20, 1984, originally leaked.
[94] 1984–1985; H.C. 302; 1984–1985; H.C. 334; 1984–1985; H.C. 354; Comments on the Consultation paper.
[95] Water Act 1973, s.29.
[96] H.C. Deb., Vol. 72, col. 1129 *et seq.* (February 7, 1985).
[97] H.C. Deb., Vol. 86, col. 316, Written Answers (November 15, 1985).
[98] S.I. 1982 No. 863, made under National Health Service Act 1977, s.121.

criticised by the Statutory Instruments Committee.[99] This was, therefore, using a circular for purely explanatory purposes.

The Minister also has power to give directions by an instrument in writing to health authorities.[1] This power is being used to require compliance with a code of practice to prevent the disclosure of patients' records to the police under the Data Protection Act 1984 without the patient's consent except for example to prevent a risk to public health or to investigate an offence.[2] The Hospital Complaints Procedure Act 1985 also imposes an obligation on the Secretary of State to use this power to issue a direction to each health authority as appears to him necessary to ensure that arrangements are made and publicised for dealing with hospital patients' complaints. The use of a direction is, however, very exceptional.[3] The normal relationship between the D.H.S.S. and the health authorities is one of advice and guidance issued in the form of circulars, Health Service Notices and Family Practitioner Notices sometimes accompanied by a memorandum of guidance. Thus restrictions on the treatment of overseas patients by family doctors, dentists and opticians (as distinct from charges for treatment in hospitals) were laid down in guidelines to family practitioners' committees who administer the provision of medical, dental and ophthalmic services.[4] Again the controversial advice that doctors in exceptional circumstances could prescribe contraceptives to girls under 16 without their parents' knowledge or consent[5] was contained in a memorandum of guidance.[6] Similarly, the code of practice regulating transplants of organs from dead people is contained in non-statutory guidelines.[7] Following a highly critical report by the Public Accounts Committee on redundancy pay for N.H.S. employees retiring early, the Minister issued a circular to Regional and District health authorities laying down restrictions.[8] The highly controversial issue of urging health authorities to put their ancillary services out to

[99] H.C. Deb., Vol. 27, col. 257 (July 6, 1982).
[1] National Health Service Act 1977, s.17.
[2] H.C. Deb., Vol. 61, col. 217 (June 5, 1984).
[3] Christopher Ham, *Policy-making in the N.H.S.*, p. 185 quotes a direction given to the Leeds Regional Hospital Board which was the only occasion when such a direction was issued to the Board.
[4] Health Circular W.H.C. 84/11.
[5] See *Gillick* v. *West Norfolk A.H.A.* [1985] 3 W.L.R. 830.
[6] H.N.(80) 46, a revised version of H.S.C. (I.S.) 32.
[7] H.C. Deb., Vol. 38, col. 485, Written Answers (March 10, 1983).
[8] Health Circular H.C. 84/11.

private tender has been dealt with by a circular asking the authorities to submit plans to put all their services out to tender.[9]

This circular and the related policy that authorities may not include fair wages clauses in contracts with private firms has led to a great deal of resistance but the Minister has not so far seen the need to use legislative powers. However, the Minister has other means at his disposal apart from those already mentioned to induce compliance, most importantly through control over finance. The Minister has control over the total budgets of health authorities and he also has power to give directions as to the application of the funds.[10] In the last resort if members of a health authority refuse to budget in accordance with Government limits they can be directed to do so and failure to obey can lead to dismissal and the appointment of new members.[11] Where local authorities want to dismiss members appointed by them they can do so now only with the consent of the Secretary of State.[12] The ultimate power is, of course, to promote legislation and the controversial subject of private patients has undergone the game of party political ping-pong, each government repealing and replacing the legislation of its predecessor.[13]

Though the relationship between central government and local authorities, nationalised industries and health authorities respectively varied in many respects, the common feature was that normally it was based on persuasion and non-statutory guidelines rather than legal powers and duties, but, as the Conservative Government of the 1980s is tightening its grip over local government, the nationalised industries and the National Health Service, the use of legal powers has increased to a marked degree.

Central government. The voluntary approach in the context of central government refers to the use of non-legal rules made by government departments addressed to their own civil servants to

---

[9] Health Circular H.C. 83/24.

[10] Health Services Act 1980, s.6, tightening the provisions in the 1977 Act.

[11] *Ibid.* and s.85 of the 1977 Act. When the Minister used his emergency powers under s.86 of the 1977 Act for this purpose his direction was declared invalid by the court and the National Health Service (Invalid Direction) Act 1980 had to be passed. Removal was threatened again in the case of the West Lambeth Health Authority—*The Guardian*, July 11, 1985.

[12] S.I. 1985 No. 1067.

[13] The original provision dealing with private patients, s.5 of the National Health Service Act 1946 was repealed by the Health Service and Public Health Act 1968, s.3. This was superseded by the Health Services Act 1976 (consolidated in the National Health Service Act 1977), which was in turn repealed by the Health Services Act 1980.

structure discretion derived from statute or the prerogative in preference to statutory rules. Pressure to translate such informal rules into statutory form and make them legally binding on the government may be resisted on purely practical grounds, or for reasons of justiciability. Where the government has given way to pressure, informal rules to supplement the statutory ones may continue. In other cases non-legal rules effectively supplant rather than supplement the legal rules.

Supplementary benefit provides a good illustration where non-statutory guidelines have been translated into legal rules which have then been supplemented by further guidance. Before the system was reformed by the Social Security Act 1980, the wide discretionary powers of the Supplementary Benefits Commission were structured by the notorious unpublished "A" Code in accordance with which supplementary benefit officers exercised their discretion to pay benefit. Criticism centred on the secrecy of the code because applicants could not find out the criteria and supplementary benefit appeal tribunals were not always aware that they had to exercise their own discretion. When the scheme was being reviewed and a more precise definition of the rules of entitlement was recommended, it was suggested that the rules could be laid down in regulations or that the more detailed rules could be included in a code.[14] Following existing precedents the code would not be fully binding but the adjudicating authorities would be required to have regard to it. The Departmental review team saw great advantage in a code of practice as it could be changed without laying amending regulations but since it envisaged such a code as being laid before Parliament, the difference in procedure between amending the code or regulations would be purely technical. A more substantial difference would lie in the non-technical language in which the code could be drafted in contradistinction to regulations. This advice was not followed. The regulations drawn up under the Social Security Act 1980 were very detailed and had to be amended very soon after the Act was passed. The regulations are supplemented by published guidance on their interpretation from the Chief Adjudication Officer (C.A.O.) but the ultimate decision on interpretation will be with the adjudicating authorities. The "A" Code has been replaced by the "S" Manual which has been published apart from instructions about fraud and other confidential matters. This manual now incorporates the C.A.O.'s guidance as well as the Department's instructions and

---

[14] *Social Assistance*, Chap. 3.12 *et seq.*

advice to its staff. It therefore is the document which structures such residual discretion as is left in administering supplementary benefit.[14a]

It is interesting to contrast the development of internal rules in the case of supplementary benefit with that in immigration. So far as aliens were concerned admission was granted in accordance with instructions to immigration officers by the Home Secretary which were not published.[15] In the case of Commonwealth immigrants, the instructions to immigration officers were published when the Commonwealth Immigrants Act 1962 was before Parliament and they were laid before Parliament.[16] There were also supplementary instructions on matters of detail and procedure which were not published.[17] When appeal bodies were set up under the Immigration Appeals Act 1969, these rules were made binding on them[18] but there was no statutory provision for making such rules and laying them before Parliament until the Immigration Act 1971, s.3. Unlike Supplementary Benefit Regulations these rules, though subject to parliamentary procedure, are not statutory instruments and their legal force has been discussed above. The Wilson Committee which recommended the provision of an appeal procedure saw no objection to supplementary unpublished instructions on matters of procedure and detail[19] and the Immigration Act 1971, Sched. 2, para. 1(3) gives such instructions statutory blessing by providing that immigration officers shall exercise their functions in accordance with instructions (not inconsistent with the immigration rules) given by the Secretary of State and similarly, medical officers shall act in accordance with such instructions. Such instructions do not have to be published or laid before Parliament but some have been leaked to the media or come to light by other means.[20] Thus secret guidance about when to allow foreign men into the country to live with British wives or fiancées was leaked to *The Guardian*[21] and seemed to be biased to refuse entry. Even more controversial was the secret instruction which came to light when the American black power advocate,

---

[14a] The Social Security Act 1986, s.33(10) provides that officers awarding discretionary payments for special needs from the social fund shall act in accordance with directions from the Secretary of State which will be binding and shall take into account guidance issued by him. The directions and guidance will be published but there is no provision for parliamentary control.
[15] Aliens Order 1953 (No. 1671), reg. 30(2).   [16] Cmnd. 1716 (1962).
[17] Cmnd. 3387 (1967)—Wilson Committee, para. 27.
[18] s.8 and S.I. 1970 No. 151, reg. 7.   [19] Cmnd. 3387, para. 65.
[20] See Harlow & Rawlings, *Law and Administration*, p. 545 *et seq.* for a more extended discussion.   [21] *The Guardian*, March 21, 1984.

Stokeley Carmichael, was refused leave to enter.[22] The unpublished instruction was at variance with the published rules and when this matter was raised with the Home Secretary the illegal instruction was withdrawn, but this was dependent on the fortuitous circumstance that the secret rule came to light. Not surprisingly as a result of this incident there was a call for the publication of all confidential instructions.[23] A fundamental review of the instructions to immigration officers has now begun and the possibility of publishing volumes of instructions is being considered.[24] If this were done it would bring immigration instructions into line with the "S" manual. Publication may be perilous for the Secretary of State if the decision in *R. v. Home Secretary, ex p. Asif Khan*[25] is applied. Here it was held by a majority in the Court of Appeal that the Home Secretary could not depart from a circular letter setting out the procedure for intending adopters of a child from abroad without at least giving the recipients of the letter an opportunity to make representations. In the case of both supplementary benefit and immigration, internal rules have been transformed into statutory rules which have then been supplemented by new internal guidelines to interpret them or give guidance about how to exercise discretion which exists under them or remains outside them.[26]

An area where governments have steadfastly refused to be bound by legal rules is the provision of assistance to industry. All forms of assistance, whether it is non-selective, such as regional development grants[27] or selective assistance[28] is discretionary because no government has been prepared to entrust decisions in such cases to an outside body.[29] In the case of regional development grants detailed provisions are laid down in the Act and in statutory instruments made under the Act[30] supplemented by notes for guidance to applicants.[31] The discretion was

[22] *The Guardian*, February 9, 1984.
[23] *The Guardian*, June 21, 1984.
[24] *The Guardian*, April 13, 1985. See H.C. Deb., Vol. 91, col. 394, Written Answers (February 11, 1986), for draft guidelines regulating representations by M.P.'s in immigration cases. They were debated by the House of Commons, H.C. Deb., Vol. 94, col. 952 (March 26, 1986).
[25] [1984] 1 W.L.R. 1337.
[26] As in *Asif Khan*. There was no provision in the immigration rules for the admission of children for adoption.
[27] Part II of the Industrial Development Act 1982; a new Part II was inserted by the Co-operative Development Agency and Industrial Development Act 1984.
[28] Industrial Development Act 1982, s.7 and s.8.
[29] This applies even to a Conservative Government, see H.C. Deb., Vol. 80, col. 110 (June 4, 1984).
[30] S.I. 1984 No. 1843–6.   [31] H.C. Deb., Vol. 80, col. 80 (June 4, 1984).

also delimited by White Papers preceding the legislation.[32] In the case of selective assistance, the criteria in the Act are very wide and are supplemented by detailed guidelines which are completely non-statutory. Guidelines for selective assistance in development areas were set out in the Annual Reports under the Industry Act but more detailed guidelines for selective assistance had to be unearthed by the Expenditure Committee.[33] New criteria for granting selective assistance were added by the Labour Government's White Paper in 1975 *The Attack on Inflation,* which laid down that the observance of incomes policy was one of the factors to be taken into account. But the detailed guidelines to officials administering this policy were only published as a result of a leak to *The Times.*[34]

Discretionary powers structured by internal guidelines give governments great flexibility to change the rules for eligibility without resorting to legislation or even statutory instruments. They can even accommodate changes of policy from one government to another. The Conservative Government, when it assumed office in 1979, changed the criteria for selective assistance and announced them to the House of Commons.[35] Even in the case of regional development grants it was possible to raise the minimum figure below which grant would not be paid and to cease paying grants in intermediate development areas without resort to legislation or statutory instruments, though the latter change was later embodied in the Industry Act 1980. Statutory instruments had to be used to alter the assisted areas and the rates of grant. Legislation had to be resorted to in 1984 when the criteria for eligibility were changed so as to make them more selective. The criteria are further defined in statutory instruments including a limit to the amount of assistance to be provided. Such a limit could have been imposed before the Act by the use of the Secetary of State's discretion in the same way as a minimum figure for the payment of grant was fixed but this power was never used.

The enormous flexibility conferred on the government by the

[32] *e.g.* Cmnd. 4942 preceding the Industry Act 1972 which created Regional Development Grants and *inter alia* laid down a minimum figure below which grant would not be paid. This was modelled on an earlier limit for investment grants, the legality of which was challenged unsuccessfully in *British Oxygen Ltd.* v. *Minister of Technology* [1970] 3 W.L.R. 488.

[33] 1975–1976; H.C. 596 II, p. 113. See *supra,* Chap. 3.

[34] *The Times,* September 29, 1978.

[35] H.C. Deb., Vol. 970, col. 1302 and 480, Written Answers (July 17, 1979) and see 1979–1980; H.C. 772, Annual Report under the Industry Act 1972, App. 4 and 11.

ability to interpret guidelines and to change them can adversely affect the individual who has relied on the status quo. Transitional provisions ease rather than eliminate this problem. The Ombudsman may be able to help in such cases[36] and the courts have applied the doctrine of legitimate expectation to the continuation of an existing rule as well as to its application.[37] This represents a procedural fetter rather than a substantive one and can be avoided by a *caveat* that the rules do not apply in all cases and, where the rules are not published, as happened to the notes of guidance on the White Paper on incomes policy, they can give rise to no expectations legitimate or otherwise.

Internal departmental rules have been preferred to legal rules not only in the context of statutory discretion but also to delimit discretion derived from the prerogative or some other common law power. The rules relating to telephone tapping have caused most controversy as to whether they should be legally binding. The origin of the power to tap telephones is obscure and the Birkett Committee,[38] which first inquired into the matter, left open whether the power was derived from the prerogative, the common law or neither. Sir Robert Megarry in *Malone* v. *Metropolitan Police Commissioner*[39] held, "that if such tapping can be carried out without committing any breach of the law, it requires no authorisation by statute or common law; it can lawfully be done simply because there is nothing to make it unlawful." Whatever its legal basis, it was carried on without a warrant until 1937. After that date the Post Office were only allowed to tap telephones with the authority of the Home Secretary. The criteria for granting a warrant for the detection of crime were first written down in letters to the Metropolitan Police and the Board of Customs and Excise in 1951[40] and supplemented by a further letter in 1956 but they were first published, as were those governing warrants granted to the Security Service, in the Birkett Committee report. Following the *Malone* case a review of telephone tapping procedures was undertaken and a White Paper[41] was published bringing up to date the operation of the procedures and principles in the Birkett report. The then Home Secretary, Mr. Whitelaw, firmly rejected

[36] *Supra,* chap. 3.
[37] *R.* v. *Home Secretary, ex p. Asif Khan* [1984] 1 W.L.R. 1337; *O'Reilly* v. *Mackman* [1982] 3 W.L.R. 1096.
[38] Cmnd. 283 (1957).
[39] [1979] 2 W.L.R. 700, 733–4.
[40] Cmnd. 283, para. 64.
[41] Cmnd. 7873 (1980).

Megarry's *cri de coeur* that "telephone tapping is a subject which cries out for legislation,"[42] because, "if the power to intercept were to be regulated by statute, then the courts would have power to inquire into the matter and to do so, if not publicly, then at least in the presence of the complainant."[43] Several attempts were made subsequently in Parliament to embody the non-statutory criteria into statute and make interceptions falling outside them a criminal offence.[44] The Government resisted this on each occasion on the same ground that secrecy was essential for telephone tapping and that, if the criteria were embodied in statute, they would be open to scrutiny. Even if the proceedings were in camera, the suspect would still obtain the information on which the warrant was based. The Government's view prevailed in 1981[45] on the Report Stage of the Bill, reversing its defeat in Standing Committee, but in 1984, after its defeat in the House of Lords on the Telecommunications Bill, it secured the removal of the new clause only in return for a promise to legislate in the next session of Parliament.[46]

In the meanwhile the European Court of Human Rights unanimously ruled in favour of *Malone*.[47] The Government was held to be in breach of Article 8[48] of the European Convention on Human Rights. The court asserted in ringing tones,

> "In the opinion of the Court, the law of England and Wales does not indicate with reasonable clarity the scope and manner of exercise of the relevant discretion conferred on the public authorities. To that extent, the minimum degree of legal protection to which citizens are entitled under the rule of law for a democratic society is lacking."[49]

The Government responded with the Interception of Communications Act 1985. This makes interception of a communication without a warrant a criminal offence (section 1). It sets out the broad categories of cases for which the Secretary of State may issue a warrant, *i.e.* national security, prevention or

---

[42] *op. cit.* p. 733 D.
[43] H.C. Deb., Vol. 982, col. 207 (April 1, 1980).
[44] See British Telecommunications Bill, Standing Committee B, col. 398, (February 12, 1981), and H.L. Deb., Vol. 448, col. 632 *et seq.* (February 21, 1984) Committee Stage of the Telecommunications Bill.
[45] H.C. Deb., Vol. 2, col. 536 (April 1, 1981).
[46] H.L. Deb., Vol. 449, col. 1032 *et seq.* (March 19, 1984).
[47] Vol. 82 (1984).
[48] "Everyone has the right to respect for his private and family life, his home and his correspondence."
[49] *Ibid.* p. 36.

detection of serious crime which is further defined in a later section (section 10(3)) and to safeguard the economic well-being of the United Kingdom provided the information relates to persons outside the British Islands. Further definition is to be found in the White Paper[50] preceding the Act but not in the Act itself. Whether a warrant has been legally issued in accordance with the provisions of the Act is not justiciable. The only remedy for a person who suspects that his telephone has been tapped is to apply to a Tribunal of lawyers who can quash a warrant if they find that a warrant has been issued in contravention of the Act (section 7).[51] Their decision is not subject to appeal and cannot be questioned in any court.[52] They cannot tell the applicant if they discover that his telephone has been tapped without a warrant, though this is a criminal offence. Thus the broad criteria for the issuing of warrants have been embodied in law and the Government has complied with the judgment of the European Court without making the guidelines justiciable in court.

An area where there was resistance on practical grounds to the embodiment of rules regulating discretionary powers not derived from statute in statutory provisions is the Criminal Injuries Compensation Scheme. The legal status of the scheme, which originated in a White Paper,[53] is obscure, though the court in the *Lain* case[54] seemed to think it derived from the prerogative. The *raison d'être* for an *ex gratia* non-statutory scheme was the ability "to go ahead quickly, without legislation, on a flexible and experimental basis."[55] It was intended as a pilot scheme but the pilot scheme has now lasted twenty years. In 1974 when the scheme was revised, following an Interdepartmental Working Party,[56] the then Government again refused to introduce legislation until the revised scheme had been tried and tested.[57] It was not until December 1983 that the present Government declared itself willing to make the scheme statu-

---

[50] Cmnd. 9438.   [51] Applying the principles applicable to judicial review.
[52] s.7(8). It would also now be impossible to challenge the issue of a warrant in court, as Malone did, as a result of s.9, which prevents evidence being brought of an offence under s.1 or that a warrant has been issued. Similarly, the warrant unsuccessfully challenged by C.N.D. predated the Act. The Court held that ministers must observe their own non-statutory guidelines but had done so: *The Guardian* September 3, 1986.
[53] Cmnd. 2323 (1964).   [54] [1967] 3 W.L.R. 348, 357.
[55] H.C. Deb., Vol. 694, col. 1138 (May 5, 1964).
[56] H.C. Deb., Vol. 971, col. 17, Written Answers (July 23, 1979).
[57] Council on Tribunals, Annual Report for 1979–1980, Chap. 2.10.
[58] H.L. Deb., Vol. 446, col. 283 *et seq.* (December 14, 1983).

tory.[58] As was pointed out in the same debate, flexibility could be preserved by a short enabling Act giving power to the Home Secretary to embody the scheme in a statutory instrument. The reluctance in this case to legislate is not, therefore, based, as in the case of telephone tapping, on opposition to opening the scheme to judicial review, which has been in existence since the *Lain* case in 1967. The obstacles to legislation have been purely pragmatic but they have not yet been overcome.

The rationale for extra-statutory tax concessions is also purely practical. Class concessions, which apply generally to groups of taxpayers, are constantly reviewed under pressure from the Comptroller and Auditor General and the Public Accounts Committee with a view to placing them on a statutory basis. Both the Inland Revenue Board and the Customs and Excise Commissioners have been regularly examined about their success in reducing the tally of class concessions.[59] The reasons for not legislating in the case of certain concessions are a variety of practical factors. One of the main problems is finding parliamentary space in the Finance Bill. The Public Accounts Committee has suggested that concessions could be included in non-controversial Bills and sent to a Second Reading Committee.[60] There may also be problems inherent in the concessions themselves which make them unsuitable for legislation. They may be trivial or transient (though some of these may be of long standing).[61] They may be very detailed and require complex legislation which would not be warranted in the circumstances. It may also be desirable to give the concession a reasonable run before legislating[62] and some may be subject to frequent variations. The Public Accounts Committee has met this argument by recommending that legislation could provide for the making or varying of concessions by statutory instrument.[63] This solution was adopted in the Finance Act 1968[64] for the baggage concessions for travellers' luggage operated by the Commissioners for Customs and Excise, though they had earlier told the Public Accounts Committee that this was not possible.[65] When it was suggested to them that this precedent could be used for other cases, the width of power needed to be delegated was

---

[59] See 1966–1967; H.C. 647 para. 7 *et seq.*; 1968–1969; H.C. 188–I, para. 1 *et seq.*; 1981–1982; H.C. 339, para. 29 *et seq.*
[60] 1981–1982; H.C. 339, para. 33.
[61] *Ibid.* para. 32.
[62] 1970–1971; H.C. 300–I, Q.3382.
[63] 1968–1969; H.C. 185–I, para. 1.
[64] s.7.   [65] 1966–1967; H.C. 647, Q.2613.

raised, to which the obvious reply was made that wide statutory authority was better than none.[66]

A different problem arises where a concession, though general, could, if expressed in statutory form, be open to abuse.[67] This is where class concessions merge into individual remissions of tax or duty on grounds of equity or hardship or where pursuit is impracticable. These individual concessions cannot by definition be embodied in legislation, though they may show that there is something wrong with the legislation.[68] The Select Committee on the Parliamentary Commissioner for Administration recommended an extension to the extra-statutory concession to remit arrears of tax on grounds of hardship, so as to provide a financial remedy for taxpayers who sustained injustice as a result of errors by the Inland Revenue without sole regard to the degree of hardship.[69] The Government responded with a White Paper allowing remission based on degrees of hardship.[70]

Non-statutory rules which may be difficult to distinguish in practice from concessions though conceptually different are Statements of Practice issued by the Inland Revenue. These describe the way in which the Department will interpret the law, though such interpretation is, of course, open to challenge in the courts. A concession, on the other hand, is a departure from the strict letter of the law in favour of the taxpayer.[71]

Conventions may also be in conflict with the strict letter of the law but their embodiment in law raises fundamental rather than practical issues. These were addressed by the Committee of Privy Councillors who were asked to report on the rules which should govern the publication of ministerial memoirs[72] following the *Crossman Diaries* Case.[73] The Committee in criticising the existing law expressed the view that a judge is not likely to be so equipped as to make him the best arbiter of the political and administrative issues involved.[74] Their objection to the introduction of legislation is worth quoting in full,

---

[66] 1968–1969; H.C. 185–I, Q.3003 *et seq.*

[67] For examples, see *ibid.* App. 5.

[68] *Absalom* v. *Talbot* [1943] 1 All E.R. 589, 598A. See 1981–1982; H.C. 339, Q.2216 for the danger of using concessions as a way to avoid the difficulties of drafting legislation.

[69] 1970–1971; H.C. 240, para. 12.

[70] Cmnd. 4729 (1971).

[71] 1981–1982; H.C. 76–ix, para. 70.

[72] Cmnd. 6386 (1976).

[73] *Att.-Gen.* v. *Jonathan Cape* [1975] 3 W.L.R. 606.

[74] *op. cit.*, para. 66.

"While we are satisfied that the public interest calls for some workable restrictions in this field, they seem to us remote from any true connection with the concepts of criminal law. It is to be remembered that in all we are speaking of the occasional and limited activities of a small number of persons; and those persons men or women who *ex hypothesi* have held high office under the Crown and responsible positions in public life. They should be able, surely, to conduct themselves properly and recognise their obligations without the creation of statutory offences or statutory penalties. To be driven to suggest otherwise would be to acknowledge a sad decline in the prestige of modern government. We do not think that things have come to such a pass. There can indeed be no guarantee that there will never be anything to complain of in the future if the burden of compliance is left to rest on the free acceptance of an obligation of honour. There may well be an occasional rebel or an occasional breach; but so long as there remains a general recognition of the practical necessity of some rules and the importance of observing them, we do not think that such transgressions, even though made the subject of sensational publicity, should be taken as having shattered the fabric of a sensible system."[75]

This passage could serve as a classic justification for the existence of the conventions of the constitution which epitomise the voluntary approach, as the bedrock of the Constitution in preference to law. The Committee recommended that a memorandum abstracting the substance of the Report be circulated to all incoming ministers and that they should sign a declaration that it had been drawn to their attention. This was accepted by the Government of the day.[76] However, this case illustrates that the formulation of a voluntary code may be the result of a breach of the rules on which the code itself is based.[77] The extent to which the effectiveness of the voluntary approach is dependent on acceptance and trust will now be examined.

---

[75] *op. cit.*, para. 69.

[76] H.C. Deb., Vol. 903, col. 521, Written Answers (January 22, 1976).

[77] Another example is the guidance issued by the Head of the Civil Service about the duties and responsibilities of civil servants in relation to ministers (H.C. Deb., Vol. 68, col. 130, Written Answers (February 26, 1985)) as a result of the *Ponting* Case; see further below, p. 104.

Chapter 6

CONCLUSION

There are certain recurrent themes which run through the plethora of quasi-legal or purely voluntary rules which have been categorised in the foregoing pages and they provide the rationale for the use of this mechanism in a vast variety of situations.

Perhaps the most obvious and commonest justification for the use of non-legal rules is the ability to use non-technical language. The precise legal language in which statutes and statutory instruments are couched so that the courts will not be able to misunderstand the will of the legislature, forms an enormous obstacle to understanding and use which can be circumvented by the use of informal rules written in ordinary every day language and not given direct legal force. The advantages of being able to use the language of exhortation and advice, the comparative ease and speed with which such rules can be drafted and their comprehensibility to the layman are constantly stressed. It is a common denominator running through all informal rules but it has received particular emphasis in some cases. Particular illustrations where this factor has been highlighted are the Highway Code, the Health and Safety Codes, the Industrial Relations Code, the codes of practice under the Police and Criminal Evidence Act 1984, the codes of practice in relation to planning procedures, the Immigration Rules, the Criminal Injuries Compensation Scheme and certain tax concessions. When the supplementary benefit scheme was being reviewed, the departmental review team pointed out the advantages of a code of practice over regulations on this ground amongst others but its advice was not followed and very complex regulations have been the result.

Very closely connected with the informal language of such rules is their flexibility. The ability to change rules easily and quickly is another common denominator underlying most informal rules. The degree of flexibility does, however, depend on the statutory provisions, if any, under which the rules are made. Frequently, as we have seen, statutes provide for codes to be laid before Parliament for approval or to allow annulment and apply this procedure to any revision of the codes. In such cases codes are not more flexible than statutory instruments. The argument in favour of the flexibility of codes in such cases is, therefore, disingenuous and is really an alibi for other reasons such as informality of language or lack of direct legal force. As we have seen, in the case of some tax concessions and criminal injuries compensation it was conceded that the same flexibility could be achieved by using a statutory intrument. However, in the latter case this was only conceded twenty years after the *ex gratia* non-statutory scheme had been introduced. This scheme, which was intended as a pilot scheme, illustrates the close connection between flexibility and the ability to experiment as the justification for informal rules. The lack of scientific knowledge which made objective judgements impossible and the ability to experiment were also given as the justification for preferring quasi-legal codes to statutory instruments in the case of regulating the welfare of animals and health and safety at work. Flexibility and the ability to test the water are important hall-marks of quasi-legal and non-legal rules but these advantages are shared with statutory instruments which are no less flexible where they are subject to the same parliamentary procedures. The real difference lies in their legal force.

A third theme which underlies many of the informal rules discussed above, especially in the public sector, is uniformity. The numerous examples of guidelines to the police, prison governors, local authorities and health authorities, whether made under statutory provisions or purely extra-statutory, illustrate this theme. Guidance issued by Ministers to their own civil servants, *e.g.* in relation to the administration of supplementary benefit, immigration or aid to industry perform a similar function. Guidelines to achieve uniformity may also be addressed to private persons such as those under the Mental Health (Amendment) Act 1982 for the guidance of doctors and others and the extra-statutory codes setting standards for private homes for the elderly. Taking a wider perspective, it can be said to be arbitrary to single out the above examples, as it is an inherent function of all rules to bring about uniformity of conduct. *A fortiori* this is the function of legal rules. This *raison d'être* of non-legal or quasi-legal rules is, therefore, often expressed as providing for uniformity with flexibility. But in this context flexibility refers not to the ability to change the rules easily but to the fact that the rules are not made legally binding.

Underlying these pragmatic reasons, therefore, is the fundamental rationale for these rules *i.e.* that they are not legally binding. This is what has been called the voluntary approach. The basic reason for preferring quasi-legal or non-legal rules to law is that persuasion may be preferable to compulsion. This has

been the *raison d'être* for codes of practice not having full legal
force from the Highway Code onwards. When legislating for this
and subsequent codes stress was laid on obtaining consent.
Codes were seen as a better means of securing acceptance and
compliance than law. It is very difficult to evaluate the extent to
which this approach has been successful. In many cases the
provisions are too recent to have yielded any results. In other
cases it is difficult to find concrete evidence. There are areas,
however, where it is possible to evaluate the success or failure of
the voluntary approach. Most significant are those cases where it
has been superseded by legal provisions. They are not always the
result of the breakdown of the voluntary approach but they
illustrate its rejection.

The Code on Picketing under the Employment Act 1980 is
perhaps the prime example of a code more honoured in the
breach than the observance. During the miners' strike in
particular, though official pickets were limited to six by the
police in accordance with the code, vast numbers of miners
turned up at collieries where work was continuing. Precisely to
deal with this type of situation the Public Order Bill 1986, s.14
confers on the police power to give directions limiting the
numbers taking part in a public assembly in the open air where
they reasonably apprehend (*inter alia*) the intimidation of
others.

The voluntary approach under the Wildlife and Countryside
Act 1981 has already received some knocks. As a result of
unanimous criticism the loophole in section 28 which allowed
sites of special scientific interest (S.S.S.I.) to be destroyed during
the three-month notification period has been closed by the
amending Act of 1985. By extending the period of notice which a
farmer must give of a potentially damaging operation from three
to four months it also gives the Nature Conservancy Council
(N.C.C.) more time to apply for a nature conservation order
under section 29, where a management agreement cannot be
negotiated within the period. Both these loopholes would not
have needed closing by law if the code of guidance had been
obeyed. The code has in fact become useless except as an
explanatory memorandum of the Act.[1] In fact, however, only a
small proportion of the S.S.S.I.s which have been damaged fell
victim to the three-month loophole.[2] Though the number of sites
damaged is very much in dispute between the National Farmers'

[1] See Ball [1985] J.P.L. 767, 773.
[2] 1984–1985; H.C. 6, Evidence, p. 73–75—14 S.S.S.I.s are listed by the N.C.C.

Union (N.F.U.)[3] and Friends of the Earth (F.O.E.),[4] the N.C.C. put the number of sites damaged in 1983–1984 at 156, half of which had been notified under the National Parks and Access to the Countryside Act 1949 but which had not yet been renotified under the 1981 Act,[5] 32 of these were cases of serious damage. This represents an improvement when compared with the year immediately before the 1981 Act when 350 sites were damaged.[6] These figures must be seen in the context of over 4000 sites of which over 1300 have been renotified under the 1981 Act.[7] On the other hand the N.C.C. has not the resources to carry out regular monitoring and the figures are based on "incidental" monitoring carried out during survey work.[8] The N.C.C. are also aware of 20–25 breaches of section 28[9] and three prosecutions have been brought.[10] Whether these figures illustrate the failure of the 1981 Act as F.O.E. claim or whether this is regarded as gross exaggeration, which is the N.F.U.'s view, is a matter of judgement.

There is no doubt, however, that there has occurred a number of *causes célèbres* where conservationists have sat in front of bulldozers to prevent destruction of wildlife sites and where the Government has intervened by using its statutory powers. In other cases destruction has gone ahead. At Limpenhoe in the Norfolk Broads it approved a direction under Article 4 of the General Development Order 1977,[11] it also extended section 41 of the 1981 Act to enable objections to be made to farm capital grants by the Broads Authority.[12] The D.O.E. and the Country-side Commission have also funded a scheme under section 40 of the Act to pay farmers to preserve traditional farming methods.[13] In Craig Meagaidh, an S.S.S.I. where a forestry firm applied for a grant to plant conifers, the Scottish Secretary as a compromise approved a grant for only half the site.[14] He had refused to make

[3] *Ibid.* Evidence, p. 159.
[4] *Ibid.* Evidence, p. 37.
[5] *Ibid.* Evidence, p. 84.
[6] *Ibid.* Evidence, p. 69, para. 26.
[7] *Ibid.* Evidence, p. 76.
[8] *Ibid.* Evidence, p. 69, para. 26.
[9] *Ibid.* Q.45.
[10] H.C. Deb., Vol. 70,col. 553, Written Answers (January 10, 1985).
[11] H.C. Deb., Vol. 63, col. 147 (July 3, 1984).
[12] 1984–1985; H.C. 6, Evidence, p. 127.
[13] *Ibid.* Evidence, p. 41, para. 33 and *The Guardian*, June 17, 1985, and see now s.18 of the Agriculture Act 1986 for the payment of grants in environmentally sensitive areas.
[14] *Ibid.* Q.47.

a nature conservation order under section 29 of the 1981 Act.[15] A similar compromise was reached in a management agreement between the N.C.C. and a Scottish distiller over extraction of peat on the Isle of Islay.[16]

In some of these cases it has been alleged that the 1981 Act is a positive incentive to destroy wildlife sites by encouraging farmers to put forward proposals for development in order to obtain compensation.[17] Such claims of abuse of the Act are difficult to substantiate and have been refuted by the D.O.E. who do, however, admit that one farmer's claim may have a domino effect on other farmers.[18] This is inherent in the Act itself and the financial guidelines which allow a farmer to claim compensation for not doing something rather than for furthering conservation, though some management agreements have been concluded which further this aim.[19] It is significant that three-quarters of the sites which have been renotified had to be protected by management agreements.[20]

Another abuse which defeats the purpose of the Act is the retrospective notification of farm capital grants under section 41, *i.e.* after the work had been carried out.[21] This is not a ground *per se* for refusing the grant by the Ministry of Agriculture but it prevents the objecting authority from arguing that the site has been damaged if they did not already know the site.[22] By this means the notifications are being circumvented and this is happening in ten per cent of all notifications.

The voluntary approach cannot, therefore, be said to have been an undisputed success. Not only have glaring loopholes had to be closed by legislation but a substantial minority of farmers have taken advantage of continuing weaknesses in the Act as well as directly flouting its provisions. Most significantly its compensation provisions have been overused, if not abused, so that, although the N.C.C. claims that no site has yet been lost for lack of money,[23] the D.O.E. is seriously worried about the

---

[15] *Ibid.* Evidence, p. 69, para. 22.
[16] *The Guardian*, August 31, 1985.
[17] 1984–1985; H.C. 6, Q.47 and Q.70.
[18] *Ibid.* Q.159.
[19] *Ibid.* Q.154 and Evidence, p. 189 *et seq.*
[20] *Ibid.* Q.47. At the end of 1984, 1311 sites had been renotified and 902 management agreements had been or were being concluded, Cmnd. 9522, para. 2.4.
[21] 1984–1985; H.C. 6, Evidence, p. 5, para. 26 and p. 103, para. 43.
[22] *Ibid.* Q.118.
[23] *Ibid.* Evidence, p. 69, para. 27.

escalating cost.[24] In the most notorious cases the Government has had to intervene by using its statutory powers or negotiating a compromise solution. Blackmail may be too strong a word but the desire not to "antagonise farmers by loading them with too many new duties and controls"[25] can be bought at too high a price.

In the case of animal welfare the voluntary approach has also been under attack. As we saw, the Select Committee on Agriculture recommended more regulations instead of non-mandatory codes,[26] and the Farm Animal Welfare Council is considering all welfare codes to see whether any of the recommendations should be made mandatory by being incorporated into regulations.

In the realm of health and safety at work, the voluntary approach as recommended by the Robens Committee, has not been implemented. The Health and Safety Commission sees the statutory codes and more informal guidance as a supplement to regulations, with the advantages of non-technical language and flexibility. A more radical approach was put forward in evidence to the Employment Committee by the Chemical Industries Association who saw the development of the industry's own codes, *i.e.* self-regulation as a better way of proceeding than approved codes under the Act.[27] The T.U.C. took exactly the opposite view. They commended the Health and Safety Commission's approach of attaching codes of practice to regulations, which enabled the mandatory requirements to be more flexibly expressed, but they were opposed to purely voluntary codes.[28] These have been said to be ineffective *vis-à-vis* the small employer who needed to be brought into line with the bigger firms who were more safety conscious.[29]

A similar distinction between large and medium-sized firms and smaller firms in observing voluntary codes has been made in connection with the Industrial Relations Code made under the Industrial Relations Act 1971. The Commission for Industrial Relations study confirmed that it had little effect on small firms but considerable effect on large and medium-sized firms.[30]

[24] *Ibid.* Evidence, p. 128, para. 24. The N.C.C. has estimated spending rising to £15 million per annum in management agreements—*ibid.* Q.67.

[25] *Ibid.* Report, para. 7.

[26] 1980–81; H.C. 406, para. 39.

[27] 1981–82; H.C. 400, Evidence, p. 19.

[28] *Ibid.* Q.113.

[29] *Ibid.* p. 129. Memorandum from the Institution of Professional Civil Servants.

[30] Report No. 69, 1974 and Standing Committee E, col. 61 (May 16, 1974), Trade Union and Labour Relations Bill.

Similarly the code on the provision of information under the Employment Protection Act 1975 was said by A.C.A.S. to have had very limited influence on small firms but some influence on big firms. On the other hand A.C.A.S. thought that the code on disciplinary procedures had a very big influence on industrial relations practice and the code on time-off a lesser influence.[31]

Examples where a purely voluntary approach has proved ineffective and had to be supplemented or superseded by statutory regulation are the control of video recordings, the sale of glue-sniffing kits and straw-burning. In a very different area, the voluntary incomes policy of the Labour Government finally broke down when the House of Commons disapproved of the blacklisting of firms who offended against the policy.[32]

It is, however, in relation to public authorities that the voluntary approach based on consensus has shown most signs of breakdown. This has been most marked in relation to local government. Particularly in relation to local government finance, law has replaced consensus as a means of keeping local authorities within the expenditure targets set by central government. But this is the culmination of a series of post-war confrontations over policy; this could be dated from the Housing Finance Act 1972 which imposed rent increases and led to the confrontation with Clay Cross councillors.[33] The ultimate solution to this breakdown of relations lies in the emasculation and finally abolition of recalcitrant local authorities as exemplified by the G.L.C. and Metropolitan County Councils.[34]

A similar progression can be seen in relation to the nationalised industries. The voluntary approach based on lunch-table directives and the agreement of strategic objectives and financial targets still predominates, though resort has been had to legal directives and the imposition of price rises through the External Financing Limit. So far this is still the exception rather than the rule, but the Consultation Paper on Nationalised Industries Legislation[35] envisaged giving Ministers statutory powers to set financial targets, order the sale of assets and dismiss board members. Such a Bill would signal the demise of the voluntary approach whilst privatisation provides for the progressive abolition of the nationlised industries themselves.

The voluntary approach in relation to the health authorities

---

[31] 1979–1980; H.C. 462, Q.336.
[32] H.C. Deb., Vol. 960, col. 415 (December 13, 1978).
[33] *Asher* v. *Secretary of State for the Environment* [1974] 2 W.L.R. 466.
[34] London Regional Transport Act 1984 and Local Government Act 1985.
[35] H.M. Treasury (December 20, 1984).

has also come under great strain as a result of the circular asking health authorities to submit plans to put their ancillary services out to tender and not to include a fair wages clause in contracts with private contractors. Some district health authorities have refused to comply with one or other of these provisions.[36] If these authorities continue to hold out the Minister will have to use his statutory powers.

The voluntary approach *vis-à-vis* the police will receive its severest test in relation to the codes of practice under the Police and Criminal Evidence Act 1984. The codes are not devoid of legal effect but failure to observe them does not render a person liable to civil or criminal proceedings. Where they have been implemented on a trial basis allegations have already been made after the Tottenham riots that they were breached.[37] That guidelines to the police are not always observed came to light in connection with jury vetting when it was discovered in 1979 that one police force was breaking the Home Office circular of 1975. It was alleged that this was still happening in 1980.[38]

In the realm of central government there has also been a movement from internal rules structuring discretion to statutory rules. This happened in the case of immigration and supplementary benefit, though the discretionary social fund under the Social Security Act 1986 will to some extent reverse this trend. Tax concessions are under constant scrutiny with a view to placing them on a statutory basis and it has been conceded that the criminal injuries compensation scheme will be put on a statutory footing. Most importantly the rules regulating telephone tapping have been embodied in a statute. In the case of tax concessions affecting groups of taxpayers the problem of embodying them in legislation is purely practical. But in the case of supplementary benefit, immigration and particularly telephone tapping, the transformation of internal rules into law raises the question of their justiciability. By making the rules justiciable in courts or tribunals their interpretation and enforcement is entrusted to an external body rather than trusting the government department or minister with their application. In the case of criminal injuries compensation this already happens in practice and, therefore, putting the scheme on a statutory basis will amount to a purely formal change. In the other cases the law was prayed in aid not because the non-legal

---

[36] *The Guardian* September 18, 1984, and October 2 and 12, 1984.
[37] *The Guardian*, October 27, 1985.
[38] H.C. Deb., Vol. 979, col. 947 (February 25, 1980).

rules were not being observed but so that they could be seen to be observed by giving an appeal against their application to an impartial body.

When there has been a breach in the observance of conventions, there may be a call for embodying them in legislation.[39] This call was resisted by the Radcliffe Committee on Ministerial Memoirs[40] which was set up in the wake of the publication of the Crossman diaries. They felt it would be a vote of no confidence in those holding high office in the government if they could not be trusted to conduct themselves properly without the sanction of the criminal law. They regarded acceptance of the substance of their Report by those concerned as sufficient to secure observance except by the occasional rebel, so long as there was a general recognition of the need for such rules. The formulation of codes of conduct for those holding public office has been resorted to or suggested in a number of cases where their conduct has been the subject of investigation. A code of conduct for councillors arose out of the recommendations of the Redcliffe-Maud Committee set up in the wake of the Poulson affair.[41] Similarly, a code was recommended by the Treasury and Civil Service Committee to regulate the conduct of crown servants accepting outside appointments.[42] Most recently the Head of the Home Civil Service, after consultation with permanent secretaries alone, issued a note of guidance on the duties and responsibilities of civil servants in relation to Ministers as a result of the *Ponting* case.[43] A different code of ethics with an appeal mechanism for the civil servant has been recommended by the First Division Association, the trade union of the highest echelons of the civil service.[44] Such codes represent a compromise between legislative rules and the status quo of unwritten rules whose breach gave rise to their formulation, but they are still illustrations of the voluntary approach and depend on voluntary acceptance for their observance. Such codes can only succeed on a basis of trust and the free acceptance of an obligation of honour[45] by those holding public office. The same applies to the convention of ministerial responsibility. If

---

[39] The Parliament Act 1911 is the supreme example.

[40] Cmnd. 6386 (1976).

[41] Cmnd. 5636 (1974). The Code was contained in D.O.E. Circular 94/75. Breach may be treated as maladministration by the local ombudsmen.

[42] 1983–1984; H.C. 302, para. 3.14 *et seq.* This was rejected by the Government, Cmnd. 9465.

[43] H.C. Deb., Vol. 68, col. 130, Written Answers (February 26, 1985).

[44] 1985–1986; H.C. 92, p. 64.   [45] Cmnd. 6386, para. 69.

ministers cease to accept accountability to Parliament as an obligation of honour it will indeed mark a "sad decline in the prestige of modern government."[46] The reluctance to supply Parliament with information about the sinking of *The Belgrano*[47] and the rescue of Westland Helicopters[47a] may become land-marks in this decline, though they must be counterbalanced by the resignations of Lord Carrington over the invasion of the Falklands and Leon Brittan over the leaking of the Solicitor-General's letter about Westland, in both cases against the express wishes of the Prime Minister. If there is a breakdown of the conventional safeguards, the call for legal safeguards and a written constitution becomes inevitable.[48] This would substitute legal accountability for political responsibility. Politicians would only have themselves to blame.

The resort to quasi-legal or non-legal rules is not a panacea; it may be nothing more than a sop to pressure groups. In a number of cases the provisions for a code of practice or guidance have been introduced during the passage of a Bill in response to pressure and they may be a compromise between imposing a legal obligation and doing nothing. Alternatively, a pledge may be given for a voluntary code to be drawn up. Examples of the former are the Wildlife and Countryside Act 1981, the Race Relations Act 1976, the Fair Trading Act 1973, the Trade Union and Labour Relations Act 1974,[49] the Transport Act 1982 (guidance about fixed penalty offences), the West Midlands County Council Act 1980 (code of guidance by Chief Constable for the organisation of street processions), the Mental Health Amendment Act 1982 (guidance in relation to the admission of patients to mental hospitals), Health and Social Services and Social Security Adjudications Act 1983 (code of practice with regard to access to children in care), Police and Criminal Evidence Act 1984 (guidance concerning liaison between the police and the community in the Metropolitan Police area) and the Data Protection Act 1984. Examples of pledges to draw up voluntary codes made during the passage of a Bill are the code of standards for prisons (Criminal Justice Bill 1982), and the code of practice on private homes for the elderly (Health and Social Services and Social Security Adjudications Bill 1983). Most

---

[46] *Ibid.*
[47] 1984–1985; H.C. 11.   [47a] 1985–1986; H.C. 519.
[48] See Lord Scarman (1985) *Public Administration*, p. 1.
[49] The government was defeated on an amendment to maintain the Industrial Relations Code made under the Industrial Relations Act 1971.

controversially the codes on picketing and the closed shop under the Employment Act 1980 can be seen as a compromise between those who wanted to see the provisions in the legislation and those who did not. There is also evidence that the Animal Welfare Codes were introduced as a compromise between opposing interests whom the Government wished to placate.

The legislative history of these provisions does not invalidate the voluntary approach but it does put it into a different perspective. It shows that Governments often adopt it not purely or primarily as a matter of principle but as a political compromise. However, if the voluntary approach is to work it must be based on acceptance. This cannot be manufactured merely by promulgating a quasi-legal or voluntary code but, on the contrary, this must be the basis for the code.

The mechanisms for achieving this have been examined above. In some cases the bodies entrusted with preparing the codes are representative of the interests affected. In other cases there are statutory provisions for consultation but these are not universal nor are they uniform. Sometimes there is a duty to consult with named bodies and/or representative interests. At other times there is a duty to consider representations after the publication of a draft code. There may be provision for both these forms of consultation or neither. Where there are no statutory provisions, similar mechanisms of consultation may be adopted as a matter of administrative practice.

There is a similar diversity in the exercise of parliamentary control. In some cases a Green Paper procedure has been adopted with a draft code being debated in the House, sometimes after a Select Committee report. There is the usual variation in parliamentary procedures between approval, annulment or no parliamentary control over the final code and scrutiny by the Joint Select Committee on Statutory Instruments is confined to those instruments subject to an affirmative resolution.

There is even greater diversity with regard to publication. Not only do the statutory provisions vary from requiring codes to be embodied in statutory instruments to making no provision about publication, but the mechanisms for publication form a labyrinth of immense complexity. There are the great divisions between parliamentary and non-parliamentary papers, H.M.S.O. and non-H.M.S.O. publications, circulars which are published in diverse ways or not at all, publication in Hansard or placing in the library of the House and worst of all publication by leak or not at all. As early as 1944 Mr. Megarry (as he then was) drew attention to this problem[50] whose difficulty has increased manifold since then.

In the same year there was set up the Select Committee on Statutory Instruments based on the recommendations of the Committee on Ministers' Powers[51] which, if fully implemented and extended, could bring some order into this chaos. For the Committee recommended that the new parliamentary Scrutiny Committee should scrutinise every Bill conferring law-making power as well as the delegated legislation made under it.[52] The proposed terms of reference would not be suitable for codes which have limited or no legal force but such a committee is needed to scrutinise the increasing number of Bills including provisions for such guidance, often as an afterthought, so as to bring some uniformity into the requirements for consultation, parliamentary control and publication. The terms of reference of the existing Joint Select Committee on Statutory Instruments should also be extended beyond non-statutory instruments subject to affirmative resolution to all such instruments subject to parliamentary procedure or ideally to all such instruments made under statutory powers. It would be difficult to charge a parliamentary committee with the scrutiny of non-statutory guidance or codes and here one can only rely on conventions relating to consultation and publication developing by analogy to statutory provisions. A code of practice regulating codes of practice would be a fitting embodiment of such conventions.

Such a committee and code of practice should also be concerned with the existence of mechanisms for securing compliance with the instruments in question or for monitoring their observance, just as the Scrutiny Committee is charged with reporting on whether statutory instruments are excluded from challenge in the courts.

The reforms suggested so far would be concerned with matters of procedure rather than the rationale for using such instruments in the first place. There is a need for an advisory body to perform the functions which the Franks Committee recommended that the Council on Tribunals should perform in relation to tribunals, *i.e.* that the Council should be consulted about any proposal to establish a new tribunal.[53] This was not implemented in the Tribunals and Inquiries Act 1971, though there is ad hoc consultation wherever possible. The Council on Tribunals in its

---

[50] (1944) 60 L.Q.R. 125.
[51] Cmd. 4060 (1932).
[52] *Ibid.* p. 67 *et seq.*
[53] Cmnd. 218 (1957), para. 128.

Special Report on its functions recommended further that it should have power to advise the Government on what kinds of dispute are appropriate or inappropriate for adjudication by tribunals.[54] A similar body is needed to advise on the creation of quasi-legal or voluntary rules instead of legal rules and evolve criteria for their use. At present they seem to come into existence largely on an ad hoc basis, often as an afterthought, in response to conflicting pressures to do nothing or to legislate. If the rules are to be observed, rather than be political window dressing, they must be adopted for better reasons than political expediency.

Some criteria for their use have emerged from this study. They perform a useful function in explaining and interpreting the law in ordinary non-technical language. This is a descriptive rather than prescriptive role, though these two functions are often combined in the same instrument. Where the rules are prescriptive the looser language in which they can be drafted is a practical reason for preferring them to legal rules. Flexibility and the ability to experiment are often claimed as advantages, but ones which can also be obtained by the use of statutory instruments. The use of quasi-legal or voluntary rules in preference to law as a matter of principle rather than convenience is based on the premise that in some situations compliance can be better achieved through voluntary acceptance or by means falling short of direct enforcement through criminal or civil proceedings. These situations should be identified by more objective means than political pressure.[55] Such instruments have been used most frequently to regulate the conduct of public authorities and their relationship with the government. To be successful there must once more be acceptance. Unfortunately consensus between the central government and local authorities, nationalised industries and health authorities is being strained to breaking point in some areas. Even more ominously consensus is breaking down at some points within the central government itself. When ministers and civil servants are no longer trusted to observe conventions our unwritten constitution is under threat.

---

[54] Cmnd. 7805 (1980), para. 9.6.
[55] As was done by the Robens Committee on Health and Safety at Work in 1971.

INDEX